TOUCHSTONES

TOUCHSTONES

A BOOK OF DAILY MEDITATIONS FOR MEN

A Hazelden Book
HarperCollins*Publishers*

TOUCHSTONES:
A Book of Daily Meditations for Men.
Copyright © 1986 by the Hazelden Foundation.
This edition published by HarperSanFrancisco, by
arrangement with the Hazelden Foundation.

First HarperCollins edition published in 1987.

ISBN 0-06-255445-X

92 93 94 K.P. 16 15 14 13

To my father—
Your spirit and character show me the way.
I'll be forever grateful.

Dreams are the touchstones of our character.
      —Henry David Thoreau

INTRODUCTION

Touchstones once were used to test the purity of gold and silver. Struck against high-grade metal, they would show a distinctive mark. The word touchstone evokes spiritual images of touching, making contact, having a solid base, and being a tangible reminder of truth. We all have touchstones in our lives—our principles, a word from a friend, a favorite quotation against which we measure our own thoughts and actions.

I walked very tentatively into my first Twelve Step meeting eight years ago. I planned to learn what this Twelve Step program was about, use what I could, but not get personally involved.

Fortunately, spiritual growth takes us in surprising directions. I learned about the Steps, but I also made personal connections with others in the program. Being with other men who were allowing their lives to change under the spiritual guidance of the Steps and sharing our experiences as we applied the program to our daily lives led to my deep commitment. This program revived my flat spirit and saved my life. The combination of the principles of the program and my relationships with others on this journey caused great changes in my life.

In my daily spiritual life, I often become absorbed in my emotions and stress. My perspective gets skewed by the intensity of the immediate situation, or my denial blinds me. Repeatedly, the simple words of my friends and the Steps themselves serve as touchstones. To read a phrase or hear the comment of another person is like touching base. It brings me out of my confusion and serves as an external reference point that helps me recall the path and return to it. I hope these daily thoughts will serve that purpose for you.

Spiritual awakening reaches all corners of ourselves, including our masculinity. It raises questions and makes us see ourselves in new ways. I am deeply grateful to all the men in our Thursday meeting for the open discussions we've had on the Twelve Steps and on our issues as men in a spiritual program. The touchstones from our searching dialogues are my base, and they are reflected throughout these meditations.

The dialogue continues, and that is the life of this program. We continue to find touchstones that speak to us in our particular situations, and then we pass them on to others. As you read these daily thoughts, I hope they ignite new possibilities for you and strengthen you on your path.

This book, like our recovery, could never happen through one person's individual efforts. It is the product of our Higher Power working through many people willing to give and to believe. I am grateful to the Hazelden editorial staff for the excellent work they have done. Many friends in the program have contributed their favorite quotations for this collection. Others have read portions of the draft, added their thoughts, and prayed for me and this project. Some gave me their vote of confidence, believing I could respond with what this creation called for. Though you shall remain anonymous here, you know who you are, and I am grateful for your help. And to my wife and my daughters who have patiently supported me and contributed to this project: "Thanks, I love you dearly."

—M. A. F.

JANUARY

He who is outside the door has already a good part of his journey behind him.
　　　　　　　　　　　　　—Dutch proverb

When we see how far we've strayed from being the kind of men we wanted to be, we are overwhelmed by how far we have to go to get back on the track. Perhaps we see clearly for the first time how unfair we were or how much we hurt those we love. Maybe we see how pervasive our compulsions are in our lives and how much we missed.

That is when we are most ready to do the work of recovery and become most spiritual. It is helpful at those times to remember that this program is a journey. Although at times the distance seems overwhelming, all of us are on the path. As long as we live, we never reach a point where we can stop growing. The important thing is, we are on the path, we have a good part of our journey behind us. Once begun, outside the door, we are progressing like all our brothers and sisters in the program.

Today, I will remember it is the reward of the journey itself, not the destination, that I seek.

When you can't stand criticism you learn to be a perfectionist.

—*Anonymous*

It's human to make mistakes and to feel incomplete. Perhaps if we were all smooth plastic printouts we could expect perfection of ourselves. Each man is actually a process. We are not things, but events—happenings—and the events are still unfolding. These are our creative spiritual adventures.

We have somehow learned that openness to criticism is dangerous. Perhaps we thought someone would not like us if we were wrong, or that we would get hurt or belittled. When we live with a relationship to our Higher Power, we can stand up for ourselves. A man has a right to make some mistakes! We grow more if we allow ourselves the leeway of simply being in process.

I will not ask to have the power of perfection. I will only ask that I not be alone in the process of living my life.

Love doesn't just sit there, like a stone; it has to be made, like bread, remade all the time, made new.

—*Ursula K. Le Guin*

Our relationships are alive. We don't control them and neither do the other people involved. We certainly influence our relationships—and if we are aware, we see they also have their own yeast. Whether we are talking of a love relationship with our spouse, lover, children, friends, or parents, it is a very fluid and dynamic affair. If we are actively involved with the other person and give time and nourishment to the relationship, it will grow. But if we are passive and only waiting, the relationship will grow stale.

God speaks to us through other people. Our relationship with our Higher Power influences our relationships with all the people in our lives. Today we can nurture our relationships with time, tolerance, and honesty. In turn, we will be nourished.

May this day be one in which I give attention to those I love.

There is no method or discipline or system of any kind that can ever command the spirit to be present.

—*Tom Sampon*

A man in the process of growth and recovery asks the question, "How shall I develop a relationship with my Higher Power?" The first answer is usually, "You can decide to be open to the spiritual messages that come your way." Some experiences in life can be mastered and directed, as in performing a task or going on a trip. We can have other experiences only by being receptive. They come our way, as in the growing of a friendship or the unpredictable events on a trip.

To be receptive, we must not be so busy with what we can control that we fail to notice all the experiences which are there for us. Our senses need to be open to see what is around us and hear what is in the air. We must breathe in the beauty and pain of life. When there is a message in our experiences, let us read it and not demand it fit our narrow, logical minds.

Today, I pray that I will be open to receive the spirit on its own terms.

Be able to be alone. Lose not the advantage of solitude.

—*Sir Thomas Browne*

Loneliness and solitude are very different things. When we're lonely, we feel sad about being alone. But when we're in solitude, we have ourselves and can be at peace. Many of us have had so much pain in our relationships that we often feel lonely. Or we may have been so frightened of being alone that now we avoid it like poison. All of us have known the pain of loneliness, even while we were surrounded by people.

Through solitude we can become more fully acquainted with ourselves, develop greater honesty, and deepen our spiritual development. Each day, as we spend time alone in meditation, we make conscious contact with God and join other men in spirit who also walk this path. Even in our solitude we are not alone.

In this quiet time, I reestablish peace within and find the spirit of my fellow men and women on a similar path.

Being human is difficult. Becoming human is a lifelong process. To be truly human is a gift.
—Abraham Heschel

The processes of becoming more human, becoming a real person, and finding spiritual enlightenment are very similar. They require slow growth over time. We can only follow these paths in small steps, one day or one hour at a time. Many of us grew up in families with an addicted parent. We, too, went to great excesses and have been abusive to ourselves and others. Because of these problems, we developed a distorted outlook on life. Now we still demand quick and complete fixes for recovery.

Our program says, "Look to this day." It is a difficult path to learn, but we only take it in small steps. There are no instant fixes for any human being. Yet, when we surrender to the reality of life, we are given the gift of true humanity. We feel like real people, we love others, and we enjoy the pleasure of true contact with them.

I am grateful I can be a part of the process. Help me give up my drive to control it.

To be happy one must risk unhappiness; to live fully one must risk death and accept its ultimate decision.

—*Judd Marmor*

All of us, in confronting our powerlessness, have felt the truth of this paradox. If we truly admitted how far out of control our drinking was, would we be able to survive without alcohol? If we stopped caretaking, would we have any place in our relationships? If we let go of our food obsessions, would there be any pleasure left in life? Yet, we can see much of our behavior was destroying us. We had to let go of it to begin learning a better way of living.

We can face our powerlessness in very specific ways. Let us look at today's concerns as spiritual issues with lessons for us. Does an opportunity seem like a problem because of the risk involved? Are we frustrated because we cannot accept the limits of our control? We will face our powerlessness today in ways we cannot fully anticipate. When we are honest with ourselves and face it directly, we can take the risk of letting go.

Let me not be so tied to what I have or to what I want that I cannot lean on God's love and take a risk for growth.

In wildness is the preservation of the world.
—Henry David Thoreau

Nature confronts us with its beauty in a flower or a furry animal. The awesomeness of nature is in a lightning bolt or a majestic mountain. Every variety of tree has its own uniquely textured bark. Each annual ring in a tree trunk is a natural record of the growing conditions in each year it grew. These things remind us we are not in charge, and we are moved by the experience.

This wildness is everywhere around us, and we are renewed by it when we interact with it. At night, in the city, we look up and see the ancient moon. When we live with a pet, it reminds us we are creatures too. We are part of this larger whole. We don't just appreciate nature—we are nature. When we open our eyes and learn to be a part of it, it renews and lifts our spirits.

Today, I will notice my relationship with the sun and moon, with the plants and animals in my world.

Fear is an emotion indispensable for survival.
—Hannah Arendt

We men face fear many times in life. Sometimes it's an inner voice, warning us of danger. Some fears remain from the paranoia caused by our former abuses and excesses. In recovery, we feel many new emotions, and we're afraid because we don't understand them. Any normal feeling can seem abnormal and frightening to a man who is feeling it for the first few times. We may think it isn't manly to be afraid, so we become afraid of our fear! At these times, we need to turn to our Higher Power for guidance.

We have friends we can talk to. When we simply say, "I am afraid" to a trusted friend, the fear may vanish. Sometimes it's not that easy, and we have to talk in detail about our fear. In the end, when we submit our lives to the care of our Higher Power, we know that whatever happens, nothing can separate us from the love of God.

In my fear, help me remember the comfort of my closeness to my Higher Power and my loved ones. I can reach out, and I am never alone.

If you don't take chances, you can't do anything in life.

—*Michael Spinks*

Many of us have done things that, in looking back, seem insane or dangerous. We may have had friends or family members who got into serious trouble and frightened us by their risky behavior. Out of fear, we may have become too cautious about everything.

Our dilemma is that growth is a risk, too. If we avoid all risk, we become stagnant. Life thrives on possibilities and options. Of course, risk means the outcome is unsure. We may not get the result we desire. But not all risk taking is as self-destructive as it was in our past. Now we have our relationship with ourselves and our Higher Power. Now taking a chance may help us grow, even when we don't get what we want.

Today, let me see possibilities, and guide my inner sense of when to take a chance for growth.

All truth is an achievement. If you would have truth at its full value, go win it.

—*Munger*

Truth can seem so elusive. Yet, at times it is so simple and obvious. In entering this program, many of us thought of ourselves as honest men. Some of us couldn't bear the anguish of our dishonesty. As we repeatedly face ourselves, take our personal inventories, and hold ourselves accountable, we realize we have all grown in our honesty. What seemed honest before now looks like half-truth. It was the best we could do at the time. Our perception of truth has deepened by the grace of God and as a result of our hard work.

Truth is won when we have the courage to feel the pain of knowing it. Some of our pain has been the grief of realizing what we missed or lost in our insanity. Some has been the anguish of facing the harm we caused the ones we love, and some in admitting honestly how we ourselves were hurt.

Truth does make me free. The richness in my life is a generous reward for courage.

I should be content to look at a mountain for what it is and not as a comment on my life.
—David Ignatow

We have recognized our self-centeredness as addicts and codependents. On the other side is the feeling of peace and well-being when we are released from it. Self-centeredness caused us to take everything personally. We were hypersensitive to our surroundings, to other people, and to how they reacted. Yet, so often these things had very little to do with us. God sends rain for the just and the unjust.

When we can look at a mountain and lose ourselves in the sight, we are refreshed spiritually. But no mountain is necessary for this experience. When we listen to a friend and simply hear his perspective, when we pet a dog and just enjoy this loving creature, when we look at a sunset and drink it in for what it is—then we are growing.

God, grant me release from the oppression of my ego.

The perfection of innocence, indeed, is madness.
—Arthur Miller

We've all said, "I didn't do anything. Don't blame me; I didn't mean any harm." Overdevelopment of innocence contradicts our spiritual growth. The painful truth is, we do have an impact on other people. Many times we have cultivated innocence as a style, and it has stood in our way of being accountable.

We cannot be in a relationship without sometimes hurting the ones we love. Spiritual growth requires us to take action and to take responsibility for what we do. It is painful to acknowledge we made a mistake and hurt someone. But giving up our innocent style is constructive pain. It opens the possibility to correct our ways, make repairs, and be forgiven. Then we are in the mainstream of a hearty spiritual life.

May I have the grace to let go of my innocence by taking action and admitting my mistakes.

If I am not for myself, who is for me? And if I am only for myself, what am I? And if not now, when?

—Hillel

Some of us were treated badly as young boys and never learned how to live for ourselves. We can see only two choices: either be submissive and caretaking or be abusive and demanding. Many of us have so much guilt and shame that we feel we don't deserve to stand up for ourselves. This program demands that in recovery we be for ourselves. If we don't know how, we learn. If we are unsure, we must experiment. When we make mistakes, we must admit them and know we have a right to be imperfect learners. And we can't be only for ourselves, because that keeps us small and turns us back to where we came from.

As we accept ourselves and come to know our imperfections and weaknesses, we can understand others better. We are stronger in giving to others and more effective because we have a place to stand.

Today, even if I don't feel good about myself, I will stand up for my dignity as a man.

Once the game is over, the king and the pawn go back into the same box.
　　　　　　　　　　　　　　—Italian proverb

Much of our time has been spent saying, "I'm not good enough for that job," "She's too good for me," or "I don't deserve that compliment." Sometimes we have been very status-conscious because underneath we felt unworthy. Many of us have taken either superior or inferior roles with everyone we've dealt with. We ended up with no one who could be our peer or our friend.

True humility occurs when we stop shaming or inflating ourselves and begin accepting ourselves as no worse and no better than anyone else. Then all people are our peers. At our meetings, our powerlessness puts us all in the same box. In the sight of God we are all equal—and status games which have seemed so important are ultimately silly.

Today, I will remember we are all brothers and sisters in the sight of God.

What lies behind us and what lies before us are
tiny matters compared to what lies within us.
—*Ralph Waldo Emerson*

What good qualities lie within us? How do we choose to use them today? These simple questions point our way. Yet, on some days it seems so easy to get swept along with thoughts of future pain. And when we are not worrying about the future, we may fall into regrets about the past. Either way, we are distracted from our only opportunity to make a real difference—to be the kind of men we want to be in this moment, to learn from today's experiment in living.

On this day, I will walk a little slower and will listen closely to the messages within me.

Wherever I found the living, there I found the will to power.
—*Friedrich Nietzsche*

It has been said that addiction and codependency are problems of power. Recovery certainly calls us to admit the limits of our power. Yet, to reach for power seems to come from the deepest part of our nature. If this is so, can it be all bad? Men have used power in many ways for the good of all people. We have been defenders, protectors, and active community servants. At our best, we have taken strong stands for what was right.

We need not shun all power, but rather we learn to use it wisely. Our blindness to the limitations of power created great problems in our lives. Then we learned our first lessons about powerlessness. As humble men, we know we can be wrong, but we cannot be passive and still continue to grow.

I pray for guidance as I learn to assert my strength and power for the cause of well-being.

*Communication leads to community—that is, to
understanding, intimacy, and mutual valuing.*
—Rollo May

We have all thought, "If I tell the innermost things
about myself, I will be rejected or put down." Most
real communication actually creates the opposite of
what we fear. In this program, when we lowered our
barriers and let our brothers and sisters know us better, they liked us more and our bonds became stronger. Are we concerned today about an intimate
relationship? The way to deepen intimacy is to let
ourselves be known. When talking about feelings,
we need to emphasize those that make us feel most
vulnerable.

The other side of communication is listening. In listening, our task is to hear without judgment and without trying to provide an answer or a cure for every
pain. To express ourselves to others, to be fully understood, and to know we are understood will lift our
hope and self-esteem.

---

*Today, I can make contact with people in my life by
revealing my feelings to them and listening to what they
are saying.*

Self-realization is not a matter of withdrawal from a corrupt world or narcissistic contemplation of oneself. An individual becomes a person by enjoying the world and contributing to it.
—Francine Klagsbrun

After we admitted our self-destructive patterns and gave them up, there were many days when we said, "Now what? Is that all there is? I need some answers. How should I live? How can I feel whole? How can I feel like a real person?" These questions may feel too painful to answer. These are among the first spiritual questions we encounter in recovery, and we must not hide or escape from them. They are valuable to us, and we need to follow their urgings.

We are asking these questions as if they were new and unique. But through the centuries many people have asked them too. They found answers we can learn from. They tell us to get engaged with life, take time for reflection, learn to enjoy it where we can, and try to make a contribution.

Today, I will listen to my questions and doubts as urgings from my Higher Power, pushing me to grow. I will be involved in living.

How good and how pleasant it is that brothers sit together.

—*Psalm 133*

Men are lonely and more vulnerable to addictions and codependency when they have no firm friendships with other men. Do we have one or two male friends who truly know us, know what really goes on in our lives, what we feel, and what our doubts are? If we do, these relationships are precious. We need to nourish them. If we do not, we need to find others who might become friends. We begin by taking small steps in the development of a friendship.

The joys of sharing with other men, finding humor in our mutual flaws, and joining in similar interests have no substitutes. Relationships develop when someone reaches out. It is easier for us to do this if we remember our friendship is a gift to someone else. We need friendships with both women and men in order to be whole. But understanding ourselves as men begins with closeness to other men.

I am grateful for precious friendships with men and women in my life. They help me grow. Today, can I strengthen my friendship with another man?

There are things for which an uncompromising stand is worthwhile.

—*Dietrich Bonhoeffer*

For many of us, a time came when we said, "I'm not going to live this way anymore!" This was a deep, internal decision for change, even though we didn't know how it would come about. Somehow we had reached bottom, and we no longer debated about whose fault our problems were. We quit negotiating over what we would change and what we would not change. We were willing to put all our energy into finding a better life, no matter what it would require. That is the kind of inner readiness that finally made real change possible.

Such willingness to take an uncompromising stand and give ourselves totally to a worthwhile cause is a model for our lives. It's the beginning of deep change. Many men and women have taken similar heroic stands for other causes, like world peace, compassion for the poor and hungry, human rights, and protection of the environment.

On this day, I will take a stand for what is worthwhile.

The human heart in its perversity finds it hard to escape hatred and revenge.
　　　　　　　　　　　　　　　—Moses Luzzatto

This program promises many rewards for those who follow it, but it does not promise to be easy. We search our conscience for resentments and face them. No man can progress in his recovery while holding onto resentments, old angers, and hatreds. When we hold them, we protect dark corners of our souls from the renewal we need. As we allow ourselves to be made new through this program, we no longer reserve those small corners for the game of power and resentment. They will eventually consume us and justify in our minds a return to the old patterns.

Nothing can be held back. We must be willing to surrender all—even if we do not know how. No one can stop being resentful simply by deciding to stop. When we are willing to be honest, to be humble, to be learners, to be led in a constructive direction, to allow time to be guided rather than seek instant cure, then we will learn trust and will surely make progress.

I do not need to know exactly how to let go of my resentments or what will happen after I do. I simply must be ready to let them go.

Spontaneity is the quality of being able to do something just because you feel like it at the moment, of trusting your instincts, of taking yourself by surprise and snatching from the clutches of your well-organized routine a bit of unscheduled pleasure.
— *Richard Iannelli*

The idea of turning our lives and our will over to the care of God is a very revolutionary thing to do. We are being told, "Let go of your excessive carefulness. Let the spirit guide you." When we are in touch with ourselves, with the people around us, with God, we are free to experiment. We don't learn from doing the same things correctly again and again. We learn from trying new things and making mistakes.

Overcontrol is spiritually deadening. This is a program of life. Our renewal is a miraculous event. Why stop now? We can be in touch with the messages around us without trying to control the outcome. When we let God do the worrying, we find many possibilities open up.

As this adventure of life unfolds, I will not shy away from it.

You have got to know what it is you want, or someone is going to sell you a bill of goods somewhere along the line that can do irreparable damage to your self-esteem, your sense of worth, and your stewardship of the talents that God gave you.

—*Richard Nelson Bolles*

In recovery, getting to know ourselves sometimes means developing a new form of toughness. As we deepen our relationships with ourselves, we have a clearer sense of what we care about, what is truly important, and what is not. Certainly we have learned there is evil in the world. Harm does come to good people and the good side does not always win. So we must be men who know ourselves and are not pushovers when our basic values and needs are challenged. We leave room for being wrong, and we continue to grow and learn. But we stand up for what we believe as we see it today.

We must not join the forces that would put us down or destroy us. Those negative forces are within us more often than they are outside. Wherever they come from, knowing clearly what we want and care about is our strongest defense.

I will seek the wisdom to know my values and the strength to defend my beliefs.

A richer, more fulfilling, and more peaceful masculine spirituality will depend in no small measure upon new ways of learning to be sexual.

—James B. Nelson

For most men, sexuality is one of the central issues in recovery. Our addictive and codependent lives have been fed by an overemphasis on genital sexuality, satisfaction, and performance. Sex is so limited by this emphasis that many men have become more unhappy while becoming sexual athletes.

We need to learn how to deepen our sexual experiences. We can allow ourselves the vulnerability of learning from our partners. We need to know how they relate to us, and how we can have both a spiritual and a physical connection. We can allow ourselves to be in loving relationships and enjoy the pleasure of touch. Consummation may not always be in orgasm, but in intimacy.

Today, I may experience my sexuality in many ways. My spiritual growth cannot be separated from how I learn to be sexual.

Within every man there is the reflection of a woman, and within every woman there is the reflection of a man. Within every man and woman there is also the reflection of an old man and an old woman, a little boy and a little girl.
— *Hyemeyohsts Storm*

This Cheyenne teaching reminds us of our connections—inside ourselves and with other people. Reading this passage, we are seeing it partly with the eyes of that small child who first learned to read. And perhaps, looking in the mirror today, we can see the traces of the old men we are becoming. We have been close to our mothers or sisters or lovers and have found parts of ourselves in them. By gently welcoming the children we once were, the old men we will be, the part of us that has a woman's outlook, we become wiser, stronger, more spiritual.

We don't need to be frightened or disrespectful of the parts of ourselves that don't feel 100 percent virile. We can have virility and many other sides too. Such awareness creates peace with ourselves.

I will notice the reflection of small children in old faces, old people in children's faces, and men and women in each other.

When nobody around you seems to measure up, it's time to check your yardstick.
—*Bill Lemley*

Being overcritical and irritable has been common to most of us. Some of us go around with controlled smiles while underneath we are grumbling. Others blast everyone around them. Some of us save our most critical reactions for those we love while staying sweet and friendly with the outside world. In any case, we are caught in a blinding trap. We may know we feel trapped but do not see that our problem is mainly with ourselves.

We need to look at our relationships. Have we been falling into a pattern where no one seems to measure up? Are we also being too critical or demanding of ourselves? Perhaps we don't need to lower our standards so much as to hold them less tightly. If we can be friends to ourselves and give ourselves a little more leeway, we can be more easygoing with others.

I cannot force myself to be less critical, but I can let go of my willfulness so my more easygoing side comes forward. I can be less judgmental of myself and others.

To perceive is to suffer.

—*Aristotle*

As men in this program, we have given up our compulsive escapes from life. Our escapes may have been through dependent relationships with others, or with money, sex, food, drugs, work, or emotional binges. But now we are learning to live without them, and this has brought us in touch with our feelings. We feel more joy and more pain in recovery. Often the first feelings in recovery are painful or frightening.

We learn we can deal with life—all of it, a little at a time. We accept pain as part of life. Because of our escapes, our growing up was delayed. We didn't learn how to deal with our pain because we escaped into an anesthetic, a high, a relief.

Our spiritual recovery program brings us together with other men and women who have pledged to set aside these escapes. Among the many rewards is a reawakening to all of life. No longer will we filter out the suffering because that, too, is part of being aware.

Today, I am thankful for all the life that I perceive and pray for the strength to meet the pain.

We grow in time to trust the future for our answers.

—*Ruth Benedict*

When we first started in recovery, we approached it as we did our codependent and addictive behaviors, wanting to possess it all—quickly and totally—and to do it right. Some of us thought we could learn all we needed to know about recovery in a few weeks. In living with this program, we begin to see we are engaged in a lifelong process. We are in a maturing process and this program is our guide. We can't rush it or move on to the next stage too soon. An apple tree does not blossom in the fall, and we do not expect the newly forming apples to ripen before they've grown.

Our existence in this world is like walking through the woods on a rambling path. We can only see as far ahead as the next bend. We no longer seek some big moment when we finally get the outcome or a "cure" for life's experiences. The experience along the way is all we need.

Today, I will think about the tasks and rewards of this day and trust the future for what is unanswered.

Man can live his truth, his deepest truth, but cannot speak it.
　　　　　　　　　　　　　　—Archibald MacLeish

For many men, being addicts meant living double lives. There were public selves whom others knew, and private selves whom no one met. It was a compulsive world, and both sides were false. Many of us grew up in addicted families and learned this double life early by hiding from outsiders what life was really like at home.

In this program we learn to live our truth before we can speak it. It is more in our actions than in what we say. We may never know the words for this truth because we do not consciously invent it. It comes to us quietly over time and slowly merges all our parts. Gradually we begin to feel whole again as we surrender our double lives for single, truthful ones.

Let me have the trust to give myself to the work of recovery and follow it where it takes me.

The body is the soul's house. Shouldn't we therefore take care of our house so that it doesn't fall into ruin?

—*Philo Judaeus*

Some men think it is a mark of a strong man to abuse his body and pay no heed to his health. Have we done this through drug use or abuse of food? Have we misused our bodies by our sexual behavior? Have we neglected our physical condition or health because of addictions or obsessions with other people?

To end abusive cycles, we need to act in self-respecting ways—sometimes before we feel self-respecting. Recovery and spiritual awakening involve the body, mind, and spirit. We need nutrition, exercise, sleep, and health care. Treating ourselves as worthwhile men helps us feel worthwhile. Tuning in to how we feel physically may give us some direction. As we sense how we feel, do we get some physical messages to guide our recovery?

I will yield to the messages I get from myself so I can enjoy the physical pleasures of recovery and give my soul a better home.

FEBRUARY

Who of us is mature enough for offspring before the offspring themselves arrive? The value of marriage is not that adults produce children but that children produce adults.

—Peter De Vries

Many of us, in entering recovery, are confronted with guilt about our roles as fathers. We can see so clearly with hindsight that we could have been better parents. Others of us recall the unfairness of our own parents and find it hard to forgive them.

This mixture of guilt and resentment is part of the package of recovery. If we remained the same and never learned anything new, we wouldn't have to feel guilty about the past or face our need to let go of resentments. Our spiritual renewal requires that we forgive ourselves and accept the forgiveness of those around us. Even today our children are not helped by our guilt, but they will be helped—at any age—by our amended lives. And all generations are enriched when we are able to repair broken connections with our parents.

I can accept the increased consciousness that recovery brings without punishing myself for what I didn't know.

To be alive is power,
Existing in itself,
Without a further function,
Omnipotence enough.

—*Emily Dickinson*

Being a person, a man, in this world is an amazing gift. A spiritual awakening promised by this program is open to us. But today, not all of us feel powerful and alive. We may feel weak, inadequate to our task, perplexed, or stymied. Is this a day in which we are filled with exuberance for the gift of life? Or is this a day when we're feeling subdued by life's burdens?

Perhaps we need to evaluate our perspective. Are we trying to control something or someone? Are we acting as if the world should be as we want rather than as it is? Have our individual wills exceeded their natural bounds and spoiled the simple joy of being "without a further function"?

May I find the pleasure and exuberance today that come with being alive. The simple power to be a person is "omnipotence enough."

Compassion is . . . a spirituality and a way of living and walking through life. It is the way we treat all there is in life—ourselves, our bodies, our imaginations and dreams, our neighbors, our enemies. . . . Compassion is a spirituality as if creation mattered. It is treating all creation as holy and as divine . . . which is what it is.
— *Matthew Fox*

In our search for growth, serenity, and contentment, we can start at a very practical level. Simply treat ourselves, inside and out, and everything around us in a respectful and caring way. Many men have not learned how to do that. Some of us have learned to accept abuse and pain, or to be tough and abusive.

We *can* learn about being in a healthy relationship, about befriending ourselves and others and all of creation. With practice, we will learn more and more about having compassion. As we do, our self-centeredness and our self-pity will fall away.

Today, I will be compassionate toward each of the details of creation, and practice acceptance both within and outside myself.

Self-importance is our greatest enemy. Think about it—what weakens us is feeling offended by the deeds and misdeeds of our fellowmen. Our self-importance requires that we spend most of our lives offended by someone.
—Carlos Castaneda

Were we offended by someone today? Do we harbor resentment for remarks, oversights, or unpleasant mannerisms? Do we feel tense or uneasy about how someone else has treated us? We can probably make a good case to justify our reactions. Perhaps we are in the right and they are in the wrong.

Yet, even if we are justified, it doesn't matter. We may be puffing ourselves up and wasting energy. When we are oversensitive, we take a self-righteous position which leads us far from our path of spiritual awakening. Our strength is diminished.

How much better it is to let go of the rightness, let go of our grandiosity, and accept the imperfections in others. We need to accept our own imperfections too. When we do, we are better men, and our strength and energy can be focused on richer goals.

I will accept others' imperfections; I do not need to be right.

The human animal needs a freedom seldom mentioned: freedom from intrusion. He needs a little privacy quite as much as he wants understanding or vitamins or exercise or praise.
—*Phyllis McGinley*

The boundaries between us in our families and our friendships often need to be reshaped in recovery. We need to know our feelings are private. We reveal them at our choosing, with whom we choose. We give up on mind reading or probing because it intrudes upon another's privacy. We actively engage in our relationships by sharing ourselves and listening to each other.

A secret that makes a relationship dishonest is destructive and ought to be told. But we cannot force another person to be honest, or pry the truth from a loved one. We can only be honest ourselves and guard our own right to privacy. Intimacy is the bridge which is built between two separate people. Only when we let others have their privacy and we take ours can our relationships be more intimate.

I will maintain the boundaries of my privacy today and respect the right of others to do the same.

Behind an able man there are always other able men.

—Chinese proverb

Most of us have had a strong desire in our lives to "do it ourselves." We have had the idea that strength and independence meant we should not rely on or receive help from others. Now, in recovery, we are learning a far more mature and time-honored principle. We find strength to develop to our fullest as members of a community. Maybe we never learned how to ask for help. Perhaps we haven't learned yet how to accept it. It may still be difficult to express our gratitude for the help that brought us where we are today.

In recovery, we get many lessons about these things. If we are actively growing, we will get help from others and give it too. The rewards of recovery give us ample reasons and opportunities to express our gratitude. We are no longer loners. Now we have a network of friends who truly enjoy and enhance each other's strength.

Today, I pray for help in learning how to share my strength and to appreciate the strength of others.

We cannot merely pray to You, O God,
to end war;
For we know that You have made the
world in a way
That man must find his own path to
peace
Within himself and with his neighbor.
—*Jack Riemer*

Our conscious contact with God can be called prayer. There are many forms of prayer for a man in this program. For some of us it may take the form of talking to God; for others it may be silent meditation, observing nature, listening to music, or writing in a journal.

We have experienced the healing effect of this relationship. It has allowed us to move out of our willfulness. But we need to take action where we can make a difference. We cannot blame God for every bad thing that happens—or simply wait for God to provide all the good we want. Do we see the power we do have to influence our lives? Can we give up our resentments against God for bad things that have happened?

I am grateful for what God has given me and more aware of what I can do.

If the best man's faults were written on his forehead, it would make him pull his hat over his eyes.

—Gaelic proverb

When we deal with our faults and imperfections, we are dealing with the basic issues of being a person. We can become bitter and cynical about the imperfections of others, or we can realize every person is incomplete but growing, just as we are. The way we look at the faults in others and the way we look at our own are closely tied together. In our spiritual journey, we must begin with the premise that no person ever achieves perfection.

Perfection apparently is not what this life is about at all, since perfection is nonexistent. We are lovable, and we can love in the process of living our lives. Since we are not perfect, we have to be accountable. We must have standards for our behavior and hold ourselves to those standards, admitting our mistakes and making repairs where we can.

I will try to acknowledge my mistakes and give up the idea of ever becoming perfect.

The sad truth is that most evil is done by people who never make up their minds to be either good or evil.

—*Hannah Arendt*

How often have we found ourselves in a predicament and innocently saying, "How did I get into this?" When someone has been injured by our actions because we failed to think about them, do we take the responsibility? If a friend is unfairly treated on the job, do we take a stand for him? When we know people are starving, what do we do about it? When our loved ones say they are lonely and wish we would talk to them, how do we respond?

In this program we have chosen to live by our values. We cannot sit passively and fail to live up to those values. Each situation is different, so we must think about what is called for. When we do not think about our reactions, we are in danger of adding to the evil in the world. When we act upon our principles, we feel more hopeful and wholesome.

Today, I will be alert to the difference between good and evil in my actions. I pray for the strength to take a stand.

In the beginner's mind there are many possibilities, but in the expert's there are few.
—*Shunryu Suzuki*

As we travel the path of recovery, we are sometimes overwhelmed by a feeling of how much we lack. It rises within us as a feeling of inadequacy, emptiness, or loneliness. We are in pain because we feel like such beginners. Now we need to discard our competitive thinking, our drive to be on top, and accept another, wiser, way of seeing. The big difference is in being on the path of recovery rather than lost on some diversion, as we have been in the past. It is not important how far along we are or who is ahead of whom. The important thing is that we are on the path and experiencing the process.

In recovery, wisdom comes with staying a beginner. Then we remain open to further learning. In some sense this program and our mutual powerlessness are the great levelers. Once on the path, we are all equals.

Today, I will appreciate my vulnerability. It keeps me spiritually alive and growing.

Too much agreement kills a chat.
—Eldridge Cleaver

Many of us haven't learned there is room for disagreement in a relationship. Some men who grew up in addicted families saw a lot of pain, anger, and quarreling. Many learned to be always pleasing and agreeable, no matter how they felt. Others took it as a personal insult when someone disagreed with them.

We choke the vitality and excitement in our love relationships if we are too intent on avoiding conflict. Nothing can be resolved if we smooth everything over. Differences between people don't just go away. If we don't bring them out, they fester and create silent tension or boredom. If we willingly express our thoughts and feelings, we can learn how to resolve our disagreements and to appreciate each other for our differences as well as our similarities. If two people in a relationship were exactly alike, one of them would be unnecessary.

Today, I will try to be more open about my differences with people, not as a way of fighting, but as a way of letting them know me better.

I am not bound to win, but I am bound to be true. I am not bound to succeed, but I am bound to live up to the light I have.
—*Abraham Lincoln*

With too much focus on control, we men have been preoccupied by our overemphasis on outcomes. We say winning is everything, and the way we play the game doesn't matter. We give honor to a man who has accumulated great wealth, regardless of how he has lived. We develop sexual problems because we focus on performance and achieving orgasm rather than on the joy of loving.

As our integrity grows, our emphasis changes. It is not crucial that we always be right, only that we be honest. We do not have to be winners or high achievers so much as we have to be real human beings. Conquest is not as important as connection. We do not always have to compare ourselves and be better than the next guy. We can exchange and appreciate the communication.

Today, I will grow in my relationships with others by being more true to myself and less driven toward a particular outcome.

It is a cheap generosity which promises the future in compensation for the present.
—*J. A. Spender*

Living in this moment is all we really have. We are constantly bombarded with advice to live for the future, but it perpetually exists beyond our grasp like the carrot tempting the donkey. We are told to be mindful of our career paths, to save for the future, and to sacrifice now for later rewards. We put off spending time with our children, but later they are no longer the same children. We postpone seeing friends now and discover later we have lost our relationships.

Of course, we can't be foolish about our future. We need to make some plans and delay some immediate pleasures. But for now, we can only have a rapport with ourselves and others and experience life in this moment. The present is the only time when anything can happen, any change can occur. This moment is like a fresh, cool breeze. The rest exists only in our imaginations or memories.

May I feel the exhilaration of being alive in this moment and maintain a balance in my perspective today.

The less able I am to believe in our epoch and the more arid and depraved mankind seems in my eyes, the less I look to revolution as the remedy and the more I believe in the magic of love.

—Hermann Hesse

Men have been more likely to look outward than inward for solutions to problems. Yet this program is changing us from within. As we come to terms with ourselves, as we learn to be in relationships with friends and family, the same picture that looked so dismal in past years may look full of possibilities and even rich in the present. The love we feel toward others and the love we receive change our perceptions.

We need not expect all relationships to be alike. One friend may be wonderful as a recreational buddy, but perhaps we wouldn't talk about everything in our life with him. Another friend is comfortable and we can be ourselves with him, although he may not challenge us to grow or change. No friendship, no spouse, no one person can be enough in our life. But as a group they sustain and enrich us. We need the love and contact with them all.

I am thankful for love, which gives meaning and hope to life.

*If I truly showed my feelings, the other guys
would eat me alive. It's too dog-eat-dog out there
to be honest about the things that really count to
you. You can't leave yourself wide open like that.*
—Michael E. McGill

As we deepen our commitment to strong and mature manhood, we see a conflict between this program and much of what we learned as young men. When we drop our defenses and are honest, we take the chance of getting hurt. Many of us learned long ago that when we became vulnerable, others became abusive. It is difficult to abandon everything we learned about being nobody's fool and staying safe.

In fact, we don't have to leave ourselves wide open. We can be selective about how open we will be and whom we will trust. But for our spiritual growth to continue, we must be an open book to ourselves, to our Higher Power, and to a few friends. We must face the fear of being open to others in this program. Developing true friends is part of the change which the program brings.

*I pray for the courage to be honest with myself and to
stand up for who I truly am with my friends.*

Hatred is never anything but fear—if you feared no one, you would hate no one.
                                        —*Hugh Downs*

On those occasions when we find the bigger man within, we are more generous in spirit toward others. But sometimes we think too much about what is wrong with others and how they ought to change. That is a form of hate. If we are searching for what we have power to change in our families, in our friendships, in the world, we can learn to be big enough to set aside our fears.

Do we bear ill will toward someone today? When we are honest with ourselves, do we feel a sense of fear in relation to this person? What are we really afraid of? Perhaps the same person fears us. When we can do something about our fear, the hatred melts with no further effort. Then we are in touch with the bigger man within.

I have the inner strength to face my fears today. I will not send them outward as hatred.

It takes more courage to reveal insecurities than to hide them, more strength to relate to people than to dominate them, more "manhood" to abide by thought-out principles rather than blind reflex. Toughness is in the soul and spirit, not in muscles and an immature mind.
—Alex Karras

In our culture, being a man often means being tough, having sexual prowess, and not showing feelings. We realize in this life of recovery that those are silly and immature myths, even though we see them repeatedly on TV, on billboards, and in newspapers.

When we are told these things repeatedly, it makes an impact on us. So we need to hear from each other that this is not the way we wish to live. We don't admire these attitudes, and we don't believe the stories. Truly courageous men know themselves. They have been around enough to have depth to their souls, to let themselves love, and to feel the pain of life.

Today, I am grateful to know and share my feelings and to have genuine relationships with those I love.

Love can be its own reward.

—Arnold Lobel

The feeling of attachment, of being related, of caring about someone, is what life is all about. Before recovery, we may have feared we could not love anyone. When we feel love, we may also feel cheated because our affections aren't returned as we want them to be. Or we may think relationships are just too complicated and painful. It's true that relationships are difficult at times. The only thing more difficult is having none.

In this quiet moment, let's reflect on our relationships. Close attachments to both men and women are essential to our progress. Without them, we would not be in recovery. We don't need to say to our friends, "What have you done for me?" We can feel an inner fullness and satisfaction, knowing we have relationships we truly care about and we are accepted as we are. That alone is a remarkable reward.

I appreciate the joys my relationships bring.

He who has a why *to live can bear with almost any* how.
—*Friedrich Nietzsche*

Our sense of purpose in life is not fixed in concrete. It changes from youth through all the stages of life. Often in the transitions to a new growth stage we are most confused. In the chaotic life created by our own addictive or codependent thinking, all meaning collapses around us. At these times we wonder, "What is the point?" "Does anything really matter?"

We receive a *why* for our existence by participating in the whole of this world. We are sons, or fathers, or husbands, or brothers, or friends to very specific people—and to the rest of our community, extending to all of creation. Our sense of purpose may change when life circumstances change. We get married, for instance, and then say, "Now what?" Or a child is born, or a parent dies, or we become disabled. Each time we may be confronted again with the questions. Being open to contact with our world, keeping our barriers down so we stay in touch, restores our awareness of purpose.

May I continue to respond to the changing phases in life—and be open to the renewal of purpose which is here for me.

That's what happens when you're angry at people. You make them part of your life.
—*Garrison Keillor*

Our problems with anger and our problems in relationships go hand in hand. Some of us have held back our anger, which led to resentment of our loved ones. Some of us have indulged our anger and become abusive. Some of us have been so frightened of anger that we closed off the dialogue in our relationships when angry feelings came out.

Some of us have wasted our energy by focusing anger on people who weren't really important to us. Do we truly want them to become so important? Yet, perhaps the important relationships got frozen because we weren't open and respectful with our anger. It isn't possible to be close to someone without being angry at times. We let our loved ones be part of our lives by feeling our anger when it is there and expressing it openly, directly, and respectfully to them—or by hearing them when they are angry. Then, with dialogue, we can let it go.

I will be aware of those people I am making important in my life and will grow in dealing with my anger.

The readiness is all.

—*William Shakespeare*

Our concept of control was flawed. This program leads us into a new world. Here we meet the fact that we are powerless to change some aspects of ourselves. But we can become ready to be changed. That makes all the difference. When we accept this truth, we are already changed and we are more in line with nature and the universe.

We can't make ourselves less perfectionistic, but we can become ready to let go of our demand for perfection. We can't force family harmony into our lives, but we can become more ready to be harmonious. We can't make a lasting love appear for us on command—we can become ready for such a relationship when the opportunities appear. Do we yearn for some change? How might we ready ourselves to receive it?

Today, I will try to become ready for the help and change I most need in my life.

It is not because things are difficult that we do not dare; it is because we do not dare that they are difficult.

—*Seneca*

When we reach a stressful time in our lives, our vision gets narrow. We fail to see the options and possibilities we have. If we give ourselves over to our worries and fears, our sight closes down even further. Finally, we reach the point of blindness to reality and to all the support around us. In our fearful blindness we say with conviction, "This is too difficult! There is nothing I can do."

The spiritual man strives to keep one eye on the horizon, even in a worrisome situation. He breathes deeply so he does not tighten up or close off his exchange with the world. He returns to the relationship he has with his Higher Power, trusting the process to carry him through, and he opens his eyes to quietly take in the possibilities before him.

Close to my Higher Power, I have a place of calm in the midst of difficulty and see the possibilities and dare to act upon them.

A man who studieth revenge keeps his own wounds green.

—*Francis Bacon*

Where do we direct our energy? Are we spending time and thought on how we have been wronged? On the unfairness of life? Those who consume their resources in this way have few left for growth and development. Their wounds stay open for years, and they block the healing.

What will we need to set aside our resentments and hateful attitudes? Perhaps we have been passively waiting for the other guy to make amends. That only puts our enemies in charge of us. It would be better if we could say, "I am going to move on. The change that is needed for me to heal will come from within me. I will not put my happiness in another's hands." More than revenge, we want a life worth living—for ourselves and the ones we love. We can give our energies to that.

Lift from me the desire for revenge. Replace it with the fullness of a healed life.

It doesn't happen all at once. . . . You become. It takes a long time.

—Margery Williams

Our spiritual awakening is partly a process of becoming real. We're moving from the external controls of image and others' opinions to the internal controls of honesty, listening to our inner voice, and having true relationships. We are shedding the games that maintained our old style of life—"macho" or "hero" or "poor me."

In place of the old phony surface, we are developing a real relationship with ourselves. We are becoming more aware—of emotions, of need for rest, of violations of our values. Sometimes change comes in a flash of insight or a moment of sudden, piercing awareness, but more often it comes a little bit at a time. As we work the Steps, as we are true to our inner voice, as we keep returning to conscious contact with our Higher Power, as we get closer to our friends, we become more real to ourselves.

As I grow, I see that I was always real. I was just looking at the outside.

*Every time I close the door on Reality, it comes
in through the window.*
                              —*Ashleigh Brilliant*

In the past many of us closed the door on the reality
of our abuse of ourselves or others. We gave explanations, but our words more often hid the truth than re-
vealed it. The chaos in our lives was reality coming in
the window. Many men have come into this program
priding themselves on their honesty, but not aware of
how dishonest they were with themselves.

Honesty is a pillar of spiritual awakening. There is
no growth without it, and it begins with ourselves. We
do not define the truth, we accept it, we surrender to
it. The truth may not feel good; it can even be painful.
This is the pain of birth—the rebirth of a real man.
And the promise of this day is the reward of having
our integrity and the peace of self-acceptance.

---

*Today, I will surrender to the truth. I will accept the reality
which presses for attention in my life.*

I have never for one instant seen clearly within myself. How then would you have me judge the deeds of others?

—*Maurice Maeterlinck*

We have been given the job of getting to know ourselves and dealing with our own craziness. We aren't so good at it that we have spare time and energy left to make judgments about those around us. We are tempted to become absorbed in their behavior and choices, and it does feel like a welcome distraction from anxieties about ourselves. So we must learn to detach from the family members and friends that we are tempted to fix, or monitor, or judge.

Although we are very close, we are on separate paths in life. We were not born together, and we will not die together. We will make our family or our friendships and the world a little bit better by staying centered on our own sanity.

I pray for a clear separation between what is on my path in this program and what is on someone else's path. Then we can make good bridges between us.

Self-interest is but the survival of the animal in us. Humanity only begins for man with self-surrender.

—Henri Amiel

When we were lost in our addictive ways, we were driven by self-interest. We didn't necessarily like ourselves or want to be so self-centered. But we had no inner resources to help us escape the trap of our egos. When we were there, we could not see outside ourselves well enough to ask for help. Surrender, we thought, brought only defeat and humiliation.

The inspiration of this program brings us possibilities that cannot originate from within. When we surrender, we are no longer captives within our skins. We are actually restored to a more natural state as men in community with others, who literally cannot survive as isolated individuals. We must be a part of the give-and-take within the group, just as it has been for human beings since the beginning of time.

Today, I surrender my self-interest again, knowing I must do it over and over.

All of my life I been like a doubled up fist . . .
poundin', smashin', drivin',—now I'm going to
loosen these doubled up hands and touch things
easy with them.

                —Tennessee Williams

Every man has many sides. Some sides are highly developed and other sides aren't at all. We need not fear turning to a new side and exploring it. This recovery program has enabled us to pursue sides of ourselves that were closed before. When we were lost in our narrow world of codependency and addiction, we had fewer options. Now we have far greater access to our strength and our self-esteem, and we find new parts of ourselves.

Many of us have found relationships which were never possible before, job choices we would never have had, and the pleasure of greater involvement in life. It is reassuring to see that we don't always have to give up one side of ourselves to add new ones.

Thanks to God for the many options opening up to me in this renewed life.

Power is strength and the ability to see yourself through your own eyes and not through the eyes of another. It is being able to place a circle of power at your own feet and not take power from someone else's circle.

—*Agnes Whistling Elk*

Emancipation as adult men, seeing ourselves through our own eyes, is difficult. As children, we could have our separateness only in small measure. As men, we first bring some boyhood ideas to what we experience. We may be arrogant, thinking we already know the answers to life's dilemmas; or defiant, thinking we don't want anyone to tell us what to do; or self-indulgent, grabbing for the greatest pleasure. Those ideas delay seeing ourselves through our own eyes.

Personal power comes when we listen to ourselves and to others. To be independent of everyone may have been our youthful idea of power. In manhood, power comes in being open and honest about our dependency, yet knowing we have no claim on anyone else to make us happy.

I will place a circle of power at my own feet and stand with dignity inside the circle.

MARCH

As my fathers planted for me, so do I plant for my children.
                                                    —*The Talmud*

The first seeds of this spiritual program were planted years ago by men who also were desperately in need. Rather than restrict their attention to their own painful circumstances, they broke through to a new creative idea—it is in helping others that we help ourselves. They reached out eagerly to help fellow men and women in need. In the process they carried the message to others and found new healing relationships for themselves. This program, which is saving our lives, is here because men before us were willing to reach out and pass it along.

We inherit countless resources and teachings from both our biological and our "foster" fathers in this program. The gift of a spiritually full life inspires and requires us to do as they did—pass it on. We keep the benefits of our recovery, not by holding on to them, but by planting new seeds from our harvest for those who come after us.

I will give freely of my time and resources because the giving enriches me.

The fir tree has no choice about starting its life in the crack of a rock. . . . What [nourishment] it finds is often meager, and above the ground appears a twisted trunk, grown in irregular spurts, marred by dead and broken branches, and bent far to one side by the battering winds. Yet at the top . . . some twigs hold their green needles year after year, giving proof that— misshapen, imperfect, scarred—the tree lives.
—Harriet Arrow

We often wish we had been born into better circumstances or blame our parents for our problems. Like the fir tree we could say, "If only I had taken sprout in a fertile meadow, life would be easier." "If only I had had a better life as a boy . . ." "If only I didn't have my particular hardships . . ."

By accepting the facts of our own lives, we mature into feelings of joy and pleasure alongside our griefs. Every man has to struggle with his own unique set of circumstances, even if they are not fair. Fairness is not an issue. Reality is what we have to deal with.

I will accept life on its own terms and rejoice in it.

"Why are you rushing so much?" asked the rabbi. " "I'm rushing after my livelihood," the man answered.

"And how do you know," said the rabbi, "that your livelihood is running on before you, so that you have to rush after it? Perhaps it's behind you, and all you need to do is stand still."
—*Tale about Rabbi Ben Meir of Berdichev*

Most of us accept the standard ideas we were taught. "Men should be good providers." "We will get self-esteem from hard work." "It is a virtue to be productive." "It's better not to have too much time to think."

A major crisis can quickly change our perspective. Perhaps someone close to us dies, and we are faced with how temporary life is. Or we have a health crisis, or a relationship crisis, or an addiction crisis. The standard ideas come crashing down. We look closely at the rush of our lives and ask deeper questions: Are we hurrying to a worthwhile goal? Or are we losing out in our great rush? These doubts can teach us personal things that society can never teach us. Wisdom comes out of pain and the willingness to learn from it.

Today, I will allow some time to stand still and reflect.

Heaven ne'er helps the men who will not act.
—*Sophocles*

Growing into masculine wholeness is a journey into greater responsibility for our lives. We have choices to make every day. Taking responsibility means choosing between the options we have and then accepting the consequences. Sometimes both choices are undesirable, but we have to choose anyway. Do I expect to be perfect in my choices? Do I demand that someone else take responsibility for me? Do I defiantly refuse to accept the options I have?

This program seems like a paradox—the First Step asks us to accept our powerlessness, then we are expected to go on and stop being passive in our lives. The Serenity Prayer speaks to us about this dilemma. We ask for the serenity to accept what we cannot change and *the courage to change what we can*. Fully admitting our powerlessness sheds a burden and frees us to go on from there, actively doing what we can.

If something is awaiting my action today, may I have the courage to move forward with it. Even small movement is progress.

If not for the beast within us we would be castrated angels.

—*Hermann Hesse*

Let's not confuse the surrender, humility, and serenity of this program with the perfection of angels. Today we are more alive because we are no longer destroying ourselves, or numbing ourselves, or shaming ourselves. We are men with the strength we need to meet the problems and excitements of the day. We may also get ourselves into trouble by our shortsightedness or mistaken ideas. That is why we need to continue to take inventory of ourselves and continue to be accountable.

We are on a spiritual path that leads toward fuller manhood. We accept the beast within. More than that, we like him and take pleasure in him. He has the same source as our spiritual strength. As we get better acquainted with him, he brings a sense of awe and mystery about the untamed parts of ourselves. He instills us with zest and vitality that we release as explosions of energy and power. He is in the music we love and in our dancing. He comes out in our daydreams and night dreams—in our labor and sweat. And he is in our trickery and humor.

I am filled with gratitude for the beast within.

A boy must be initiated into the world of men. It doesn't happen by itself; it doesn't happen just because he eats Wheaties. And only men can do this work.

—*Robert Bly*

Many of us grew into manhood with a surface picture of what it means to be masculine. We had images of tough guys playing rough, but we weren't emotionally close enough to another man to really know him. Many of us never knew our fathers' strengths, passions, and weak points. It left us with a distorted picture of masculinity and not with an inner knowing. Getting close to other men is a new experience, and it may feel frightening or threatening.

We can develop close friendships with other males and let them know us as we are, rather than as this picture we try to imitate. This kind of relationship in play and work and troubled times is a central part of our spiritual recovery. Close relationships with other men teach us confidence in ourselves and give us inner security.

I will be aware today of men with whom I can develop a friendship and will take one small step toward them.

A controller doesn't trust his/her ability to live through the pain and chaos of life. There is no life without pain just as there is no art without submitting to chaos.

—Rita Mae Brown

It is very hard for most of us to see how controlling we are. We may feel uptight or careful, but we haven't seen it as controlling ourselves or controlling how people respond to us. We may be worried about a loved one's behavior or safety, but not realize our hovering over that person is a controlling activity. We may be keenly aware of other people's controlling behavior with us, but unaware we have equaled their control by monitoring them and trying to change their behavior.

What a moment of spiritual adventure it is to risk living through the pain! When we do not seek an escape or a quick fix but have patience with the process, new possibilities often do develop. We can only let go of our control—or turn it over to our Higher Power. And we will do it and forget, taking control back within minutes or within an hour. Then we let go again.

Today, I will submit to the insecurity of a changing universe and have faith that I can live through the process and grow.

Before the rain stops we hear a bird. Even under the heavy snow we see snowdrops and some new growth.

—Shunryu Suzuki

The signals that new growth is underway are often very small at first. It's sometimes discouraging when we are trying to remake our lives and all we can see for our efforts is minor growth. That is how the natural world works, and we are part of this world. When the little sprouts of growth first develop under the snow in spring, we don't even see them unless we search. Yet, they signal the beginnings of a total transformation. Time will bring vast changes, but only little signs are showing first.

Today, we may search for signs of progress in our lives. The little things we see may signal bigger transformations yet to come. To be true to them in the long run we must accept them—even welcome them—as they are today.

I will notice the subtle movements toward health and renewal in my life. Welcoming them will encourage them.

*We all wear masks, and the time comes when we
cannot remove them without removing some of
our own skin.*
                                    —Andre Berthiaume

The masks men wear are as varied as those who
wear them, but their purpose is quite simple. We wear
masks to hide our real faces from those around us and
even from ourselves. There are seductive masks, innocent masks, white knight masks, tough guy masks,
black sheep masks, lone wolf masks, and many more.
Sometimes we want to take on another identity so
others won't see our insecurities. Or we think taking
the form of someone else will give us power over others, or they will like us better, or we can escape ourselves.

The cost of wearing a mask is not getting a chance
to develop our real personalities. What masks are we
attached to? Are we willing to give them up in the in-
terest of our spiritual growth?

---

*May I have the courage to drop my phony masks in order
to grow stronger in self-knowledge.*

There is no king who has not had a slave among his ancestors, and no slave who has not had a king among his.

—Helen Keller

The human race is a huge mixture of dignity and degradation and every man inherits the blend. We can respect the slave in us for his endurance and suffering. And the king in us earns our respect for his leadership and justice. Are we ashamed of who we are or where we have come from? Then we may have to look deeper and ask if we are *really* different from any other man.

Do we believe we must conform to some mold of acceptability, some proper appearance? Are we so focused on the surface that we miss the deeper values of our humanness? Sometimes we take on a reverse smugness and become judgmental of the person who looks successful or speaks well. We think, "I can't like him, he's in a different class." We all need acceptance and respect, and in this program we are equals from the first day.

God, grant me the self-esteem to accept the whole mixture that comes together in me and in the people around me.

One must not hold one's self so divine as to be unwilling occasionally to make improvements in one's creations.
—Ludwig van Beethoven

We addicted and codependent men too often feel ashamed of our mistakes. It pains us to admit there is room for improvement in what we have done. When we do see that our work can be improved, shame overwhelms us. Our oversensitivity to flaws puts us in a kind of competition with God. We are not yet resigned to letting ourselves be fully human—and letting God be God. Life is much calmer when we remember that who we are and what we do are not the same.

We are deeper and richer than any object we create or any job we hold. A genius like Beethoven could see he needed to make occasional improvements in his composition, and we can follow his model. Allowing for imperfection, we are better prepared to deal with it, and we are liberated to do our jobs and live our lives more fully.

I will be content to let God be God and accept my life with all its need for improvements.

No sooner do we think we have assembled a comfortable life than we find a piece of ourselves that has no place to fit in.

—*Gail Sheehy*

We usually think of children going through stages. If we talk about a man going through a stage, there is usually a tone of a put-down in it. But adults go through stages in their lives too. We have different drives and needs at 22 than we had at 16. Age 40 brings a different experience than 30. It would be sad to reach age 60 or 70 and have no more wisdom than we had twenty years earlier. An adult life crisis can come anytime. We may have grown out of a formerly comfortable job. Perhaps we feel new urgings for a more satisfactory relationship than we have settled for. From our recovery experience we know that crisis can bring growth.

Courage is required of us from the cradle to the grave. Change continues throughout life With courage, we can face our crises and the changes that come, and eventually we find the gift of new growth.

Help me find courage enough to live this day and meet the challenges it brings.

Victory is won not in miles but in inches. Win a little now, hold your ground, and later win a little more.

—Louis L'Amour

How much fuller each day feels when we can be patient and accept the inches we have progressed. Yet, we are aware of large problems which require miles of progress. We may want others in our lives to change quickly, we may be impatient with a work situation, or we may feel angry about an addiction.

Perhaps the spiritual message to us is we need to surrender to time. We are on the road moving in the direction of recovery. The forces of progress are at work. Our growth now may come in learning patience and trusting this process. Looking back we might see a mile of progress. It was made an inch at a time.

Today, I will accept my progress. There are many rewards already.

This above all, to refuse to be a victim. Unless I can do that I can do nothing.
—Margaret Atwood

Men have often become victims by seeing themselves as saviors. We forgot that we have needs too. We thought if we gave enough, our needs would eventually be met. In the process we became great controllers, not for the sake of power, but to make everything okay. We turn ourselves inside out to make our mates happy or to please our children or friends. But being a savior is a disrespectful role to play. When people became angry with us for it, we absorbed their anger and felt misunderstood.

No relationship is healthy for either person if one is a victim. We must do our loved ones the favor of letting them see our strength—let them bump up against it—even when that means we say a loud and strong no! After we have said no, our yes is much more believable.

Today, I will take responsibility for my own life and try not to be a savior for others. I won't undermine my relationships by being a victim.

It is only with the heart that one can see rightly;
what is essential is invisible to the eye.
—*Antoine de Saint-Exupery*

It has been said that intuition is a talent of women, but in this program we, as men, are learning to listen to our own inner feelings. This is a strength which has nothing to do with gender. Many times we have a quiet inner knowing of something, but in the past we developed an insensitivity to these messages. Our growing self-respect includes the ability to stand up for what simply feels right. We don't have to prove anything to ourselves. If we dismiss our own private feelings, all we have left to go on is someone else's idea of reality.

This realm of inner feeling is the realm of wisdom. It is the creative part, the mysterious part, the spiritual part. It is the foundation of honesty with ourselves. In these quiet moments, we are more able to perceive what we know in our hearts. As we grow, we respect and trust it more.

Help me respect my private messages from within.

*When a man's self is hidden from everybody else
... it seems also to become hidden even from
himself, and it permits disease and death to
gnaw into his substance without his clear
knowledge.*

—*Sidney Jourard*

A man's recovery is in knowing himself honestly
and learning to have loving relationships with others.
Many of us have had close calls with death as the consequence of our addictions or codependency. We
ignored the dangers in our lives and many of us neglected our health. We wore ourselves out and wasted
our energies.

Spiritual recovery and physical health go hand in
hand. In recovery, moving toward fullness in life, our
selves are returned to us. We leave behind our old
learning and habits because they were lethal. We are
becoming men who tune in to ourselves and to others
around us. We are looking at ourselves and saying,
"I'll work with it!"

---

*I will not hide myself; I will continue to be open with
myself and others.*

The reward of friendship is itself. The man who hopes for anything else does not understand what true friendship is.
—*Saint Ailred of Rievaulx*

The comfort of a true friend in a time of trouble, the strength we sense in being with someone who truly knows us, the affirmation of life that comes with enduring friendships—no other experience is like these. Recovery, once our addictive behaviors end, is mostly through relationships. In this program we are developing a friendship with ourselves, with other men and women, and with our Higher Power.

True friendship happens when we lower our guard and let our feelings show. It happens when we listen without judgment. It accumulates over time in many little experiences with someone. There is friendship in returning to someone when we feel offended or hurt so the relationship can be repaired—and in returning to him when we have been the offender. Sometimes friendship means humility, or accepting our worthiness to be forgiven. The development and deepening of our friendships, with other men, with women, and with ourselves sustains us in recovery.

Today, I will be true in my friendships.

Oh, that one could learn to learn in time!
—*Enrique Solari*

A mark of genuine change, after the pleasure of newfound growth, may be the regret a man feels that he didn't learn sooner. When we learn something new, we see how it could have made our life better at an earlier time. We regret being stubborn, immature, or impulsive. Now we see our mistakes in a new light and it hurts. This is one of the pains of change. Some people turn away from growth because they refuse to tolerate the pain of honest hindsight.

We need to face these regrets, but not indulge in them. We take a bow to the past and move on to live in the only place we can—the present. We can acknowledge our guilt and remorse and then turn them over to the care of God. We can't change the past, but we can learn from it. Healthy recovery means an ever-lighter load of regrets. Getting stuck in guilt over past deeds only repeats our mistakes by failing to use our learning today.

May I acknowledge and let go of my griefs and regrets so I can attend to life here and now.

There seemed not to be another living thing in all the world. There was something of bliss in this stillness, and something ominous too. It was the kind of stillness that beckons us to turn inward, toward the beginnings of our existence.
—Paul Gruchow

We cannot create profound stillness. We can allow it. We can move into it. We can receive it. Many of us have been frightened by such a stillness because we are not familiar with the spiritual moment. We felt moved, awestruck, and we may have run to escape that inward moment. Some men are endlessly busy just keeping the stillness at a comfortable distance. Many recovering men have unwittingly thrown themselves into a workaholic life because they were frightened by their emerging spirits.

We can change this pattern by allowing ourselves a little quiet at a time. At first, it may be just a few minutes alone. We may be more able to meet the stillness outdoors, or we can learn to be still in the presence of someone else. The stillness is a moment of meditation. It is contact with God.

God, give me the courage to allow spiritual experiences to be part of my life.

New life comes from shedding old skins and pressing through the darkness toward the light. Spring is the season of new beginnings and of growth.

—Karen Kaiser Clark

All of us in this program have had great turning points in our lives. In these new beginnings we have pressed onward or groped through the darkness, hoping to find the light, much like a new sprout arising from the cold soil in spring. Our recovery has pointed us toward the light. As spiritually alive men, we also have smaller beginnings all the time. Spring exists for us on the inside regardless of the time of year.

On this particular day, we can think about the changes we see growing in our lives. It may be unclear to some of us just what is changing or how. We may not be able to name the change or describe it until it's in the past. Springtime brings a feeling of liberation, and our growth in this program frees us from muddled thinking, denial, addictions, and codependency.

I am thankful for new beginnings in the world and the eternal spring within my being.

If I Had My Life to Live Over . . . I'd relax. . . .
I would take fewer things seriously. I would take
more chances. I would climb more mountains
and swim more rivers. . . . I'd start barefoot
earlier in the spring and stay that way later in
the fall. I would go to more dances. I would ride
more merry-go-rounds. I would pick more
daisies.

—*Nadine Stair*

"Letting go" is a theme with many variations. When
we live with gusto and are released to experience the
full excitement of life, we are letting go. When we turn
our lives and wills over to the care of our Higher
Power, we are freed of many cares. If we orient our
lives with a compass that always points to fear and insecurity, or to power and success, we are giving ourselves over to those forces. But we can orient our lives
to our Higher Power's care and support. That makes it
possible to drop our guard, allow for some mistakes,
and delight in the pleasures of creation.

Today, let me forget my worries and enjoy the fullness of
life.

Let no one be deluded that a knowledge of the path can substitute for putting one foot in front of the other.
—M. C. Richards

Recovering men know this path is not always easy. We usually talk about the benefits of recovery and the many promises of the program. Today, in our fellowship, we talk of the challenges we must face in order to recover. Honesty may be the greatest challenge. It is frightening to be honest with ourselves about things we have never really admitted or faced before.

Sometimes we have new and confusing feelings and think something must be wrong with us. But we may be just experiencing the logical outcome of our earlier commitment to be honest. No one recovers by thinking about it. We must actively take each Step and meet the challenges presented. We are not alone with our difficulties. We are part of a large movement of men committed to recovery, and this quiet moment is one way in which we are simply putting one foot in front of the other.

Today, I pray for the courage to remain faithful when the fears and pains of my transformation are overwhelming.

If anything is sacred, the human body is sacred.
—Walt Whitman

A renewed relationship with our bodies is part of our spiritual renewal. Perhaps we have not known our bodies as part of our spiritual selves. We may have treated ourselves and others as objects. Too often genitals were "tools" to be used, objects of our egos, or a way of taking care of someone else. Maybe we have used sex compulsively as an escape from other emotions. Men in recovery commonly encounter problems with sexuality. Those problems often come from knowing deep within that we must change, but not knowing how.

It helps to create new images in our minds. We can imagine a totally relaxed playfulness with our partners, with no goal in mind and no judgment. We can imagine our Higher Power being with us. We can imagine talking in detail with someone—our partner or a friend—about our feelings, anxieties, or frustrations with sex. We can imagine ourselves as a whole body, alone, not with a partner, and okay. Bringing sexuality into the whole of our lives is a spiritual thing to do.

May I find ways to include sexuality in my spiritual awakening.

*I don't like a man to be too efficient. He's likely
to be not human enough.*
— *Felix Frankfurter*

On our path we seek balance. Pursuing any single
value and ignoring another, whether it is efficiency,
hard work, or leisure, will make one-sided men of us.
Psychology tells us our right brain is the creative, intuitive side and our left brain is the concrete, fact-
gathering side. Spending our energies developing only
one part of ourselves will leave us incomplete. We
males have been taught we should be decisive, practical, and have our feet on the ground.

As men we are also creative and sensitive. We think
in stories, pictures, and metaphors, and we love music. At our best, we are willing to place people and relationships ahead of things and goals. When we are
wisest and most human, we draw on the many sides of
ourselves.

---

*Today, I will use both the creative, intuitive part of me and
the practical, decisive part that can get a job done.*

I don't want everyone to like me; I should think less of myself if some people did.
—Henry James

Many of us have learned to control the responses of others by always being pleasing and charming. Maybe we feel it's better to have others like us than to take a stand. Maybe we only feel okay about ourselves if others approve. Some of us have certainly learned we have a sense of power and control over people when they like us. Many of us have carried our people-pleasing behavior so far that we have really sold our souls for the applause of others.

Are there problems or tensions in our lives from trying to please someone? Is fear of criticism preventing us from taking an action that would be good for us? Have we neglected our inner voice by listening so hard to others? As we get stronger, healthier, more fully into our manhood, not everyone will like us. Some people will be angry; others, not interested. Once we have faced our own life crises, we are not so dependent on having everyone's approval.

I pray for God's blessing upon the man I'm becoming. I will let go of this need to please everyone.

As long as I am constantly concerned about what I "ought" to say, think, do, or feel, I am still the victim of my surroundings and am not liberated. . . . But when I can accept my identity from God and allow him to be the center of my life, I am liberated from compulsion and can move without restraints.

—*Henri J. M. Nouwen*

As we get more settled in our recovery, we are more vulnerable to becoming rigidly ruled by ideas of behavior, which should serve as guidelines, not moral edicts. If we find ourselves saying we *should* pass the message of recovery to others, perhaps the spirit of the program is missing. If we are telling ourselves we *should* go to meetings but don't feel the benefit, perhaps we have lost the spiritual path.

Our powerlessness is the source of vitality in our relationship with God. In the painful awareness that our will and our own devices get us nowhere, we can put aside the shoulds and again accept our identity from God.

Today, I will set aside my shoulds and return to trust in my Higher Power.

Man is in love
And loves what vanishes;
What more is there to say?

— W. B. Yeats

Throughout our lives we repeatedly make attachments and lose them. We are taken with the rich color of leaves in the fall, but we know that this beauty will soon be replaced with stark, empty branches. We give ourselves to caring for a baby, knowing someday this person will say good-bye to make his or her own life. We lie close to our lover in a special moment, yet we know that this, too, will be limited by the years of our lives.

We want to defiantly say, "No! If I can't have permanence I'll take nothing at all!" Most of us have wished we could outmaneuver life with such a power play. The loss feels so painful we might think holding back our love will save us pain. But holding back brings a greater unhappiness. When we submit to it, life is generous in its kaleidoscope of forms. Each attachment, each loss, is followed by more rewards and attachments. Loss and death itself are part of life. There is peace in accepting and living fully in the cycle of seasons.

God, help me to engage with life fully and to accept change.

There is nothing stronger in the world than gentleness.

—Han Suyin

It may take a while to learn to be gentle with ourselves. We have long-standing patterns of abusing and shaming ourselves. Maybe we became this way because we were victims. Now it's easier to attack ourselves for mistakes we've made than to be accountable and make amends. We think we deserve to be rejected if we let our friends know our deepest secrets. In the midst of stress we fly to self-doubt and self-abusing thoughts. We withdraw emotionally, we pout, we expect rejection rather than gentleness.

For today, let us pledge to be gentle with ourselves. Gentleness isn't dishonest; it isn't arrogant or self-centered. It is taking reality—with whatever pain that includes—and treating ourselves as worthwhile men. We will be stronger and less self-centered when we accept this gentleness. We will be as loyal to ourselves as we are to our best friends. Each day with this new attitude will build strength of character and wisdom.

Today, may I treat myself with gentleness and learn the strength it has to teach me.

Restless man's mind is,
So strongly shaken
In the grip of the senses. . . .
Truly I think
The wind is no wilder.

—Bhagavad-Gita

What passions have swept away our reasoning powers? What lust have we pursued at the cost of our values and better judgment? As men in this program, we know the ferocious winds of addiction and codependency. Now we are in a program of recovery, learning to combine our sensual side with our mind and our morals.

Every day we feel the winds of our senses, and they are part of what gives us life. We can let them blow and not be carried away by them. In this way we take pleasure in being human beings and men. We have our minds, our thoughts, and our knowledge to turn to for guidance. And we have our inner voice—our Higher Power—on which we can rely through even the wildest hurricane.

I am learning to make room in life for my senses, my mind, and my Higher Power.

We all carry it within us; supreme strength, the fullness of wisdom, unquenchable joy. It is never thwarted and cannot be destroyed. But it is hidden deep, which is what makes life a problem.

—Huston Smith

How does a man lose touch with his strength, his wisdom, his joy? Perhaps it is in the nature of humanity. Our most profound qualities are hidden deep. They never go away, but we cannot always find them. There may be nothing wrong with ourselves as men when we lose touch. It doesn't have to mean that we are "bad guys" for getting depressed or for feeling inadequate. Who doesn't have that problem? It is the nature of life that we sometimes feel this way. This program helps us unearth the resources hidden within us.

When we cannot find those reassuring feelings of strength and wisdom and joy, we may think they are gone forever. We even doubt we ever had them or could have them again. But they are still there. They cannot be destroyed. And when we regain contact we know they have been with us all along.

I will have faith that the innermost places in me can never be destroyed.

Shared joy is double joy, and shared sorrow is half-sorrow.

—*Swedish proverb*

As recovering men, we know relief and peace when we express our pain and share the burden of a sorrow with each other. Life is too difficult, a day is too long, to carry grief alone and keep our joys to ourselves. We have spent long periods of time in loneliness. Like anyone who has been alone and finally gets a chance to speak, we have much to say to one another.

In this program we tell our stories, and the telling heals us. We tell about our pain and unmanageable past lives. We tell each other about our spiritual experiences. We share our honest doubts and worries about ourselves and events in our daily lives. Full communication at a truly spiritual meeting includes our questions and the incomplete thoughts in our stories as well as the thoughts that are fully concluded. As we talk, we unburden ourselves and learn from each other about closeness and manhood.

Today, I will let the people around me know about my joys and my sorrows. It will enrich my whole experience.

APRIL

*Any idea, person or object can be a Medicine
Wheel, a mirror for man. The tiniest flower can
be such a mirror, as can a wolf, a story, a touch,
a religion, or a mountaintop.*
—Hyemeyohsts Storm

The ancient spiritual teachings of the Cheyenne In-
dians tell us that we meet ourselves in almost everything we confront. A group of men spending a night
on a mountaintop will each have a different experience. One may be overcome with a sense of awe, another may spend every moment gripped by fear, and
another may sleep the night away. While the mountain is the same, each has brought himself to it and has
a different experience. When we meet an animal, feel a
touch, or take a hike down the street, we see a reflection of ourselves and of humanity.

This day is a Medicine Wheel for each of us. Our
response to today's circumstances will tell us more
about ourselves. We need not waste energy judging
ourselves harshly, but learn from our feelings and reactions. Our reflections point the way for further
growth.

*Today, I will look for my own reflection in what I meet and
for the reflection of all humanity.*

The universe is the primary revelation of the divine, the primary scripture, the primary focus of divine-human communion.

—*Thomas Berry*

In this program we learn about being receptive. A man in search of conscious contact with a Higher Power can simply stand still and open his eyes and ears to creation. Forcing a spiritual awareness is mostly wasted effort. Learning theology doesn't create a spiritual experience either. We only need to see and hear what is around us. This is a vast and marvelous universe, and it speaks for itself. It has always been there, and when we are ready to receive the message, we will.

It stirs our spirit to be at a meeting and hear another man describe the awakening of his spirituality. As we men become more receptive to the spiritual, we open a whole new realm in our lives.

May my growing ability to be a receptive man lead me to a deeper spiritual contact.

If we were logical, the future would be bleak indeed. But we are more than logical. We are human beings, and we have faith, and we have hope, and we can work.
—Jacques Cousteau

What is faith? It is believing in possibilities. It is the ability to carry on with our plans or to be true to our work even though we feel discouraged or tired. It is staying active in relationships even when we receive little in return or when our friends aren't able to respond.

If there were no doubt, there would be no need for faith. Faith is temporarily putting our doubts on the shelf and working toward our goals. Faith is trusting that help and support will be there for us even though they're not in view. It is looking at a map and choosing a new destination, getting on the road to go there, and trusting the marks on the map symbolize a real place that we will find.

I will leave room for my doubts and discouragement, but I will not indulge them. I will choose to go with hope. I will give my energy to the better possibilities.

What is obvious to me is that we did not create ourselves . . . life is something inside of you. You did not create it. Once you understand that, you are in a spiritual realm.

—*Virginia Satir*

We do not belong to ourselves, but to the universe. No man planned to come into existence; he just happened to find himself here. We are the expressions of a life force whose beginnings are in the forgotten past. What does this mean on a practical level for how we will live today? For one thing, maybe we don't need to take ourselves so seriously. And we certainly are not to judge our existence. We have a right to be here, just as everyone does.

We can live this day fully and not hold ourselves back. We may work hard, play, and enjoy it. We need not rein in or attempt to control this force which so far exceeds our individual powers. Rather, today we can learn to flow with the current.

Today, may I remember my Higher Power is within every cell of my being, whether I notice it or not.

When angry, count four; when very angry, swear.

—*Mark Twain*

Feelings of anger are a knotty problem for many men. Some of us as children were injured or so frightened by an angry adult that we have instinctively avoided anger ever since. Or we have been appalled by ourselves when we lost control of our anger. Still, we are taught that it is masculine to be aggressive. Some of us have tried so hard to squelch our anger that we don't even know when we feel it. We treat anger like a rejected child—once rejected we no longer have good discipline over it. So it comes out in hurtful jokes and sarcastic comments, or bursts out of us in scary and destructive ways.

For some of us, overcontrolled anger turns inward against ourselves. We get physically ill or depressed and self-hating. Every recovering man needs an honest relationship with his anger. We must acknowledge this feeling within us when it is there. It is healthy to express anger directly, honestly, and respectfully.

Thanks to God for the richness of my emotional life. Today, I will notice my feelings of anger and accept them so I can learn to relate to them.

I had gone through life thinking I was better than everyone else and at the same time, being afraid of everyone. I was afraid to be me.
—Dennis Wholey

Looking back to the codependent or addictive times in our lives, we see with the perfect vision of hindsight. It is both embarrassing and humorous to see how misguided and deluded we were then. Grandiose images of ourselves isolated us from those around us and cut us off from true friendships with others. Many of us had strong feelings about ourselves that were in conflict—we felt both special and unworthy.

In this program we grow over time to have a more realistic self-concept. We are not exactly like everyone else, but we are more like them than different. It's okay to be like others, and it's comforting, too. Accepting this, we grow fully into the whole men we were meant to be, and we relish the joy of friendship.

May I accept the guidance of my Higher Power in developing a realistic and comfortable self-image.

Adversity introduces a man to himself.
                                    —*Anonymous*

After difficult or challenging times we often say, "I never would have chosen to go through that, but I learned a lot from it." It could be a job situation, a failed relationship, or trouble with the law. When we bump up against something hard—something that pushes back at us, our strength is tested, forcing us to draw on unknown reserves. A mountain climber standing on a safe ledge finds it difficult to move forward onto a more frightening spot. After he has completed the route, he looks back and feels good about himself because he met a challenge. We meet these challenges in many ways in our lives, and they help us build our self-respect.

Whatever difficulty is facing us today, we may have to deal with it ourselves, but we do not have to be alone while we do it. We can reach out for support while we do what we must. This difficulty is part of being human and can help us see more fully who we are.

I pray for the courage to face my adversity when I must and the ability to learn from it.

I'm not into isms and asms. There isn't a Catholic moon and a Baptist sun. I know the universal God is universal. . . . I feel that the same God-force that is the mother and father of the pope is also the mother and father of the loneliest wino on the planet.

—Dick Gregory

In this program we seek conscious contact with God as we understand God. Some people understand God in very specific ways as a Jewish God, or a Christian God, or Moslem Allah. Others understand God in very general and unspecific ways. To some, God is the spirit of group relationships, the deeper consciousness of each man, or the whole of creation. When the word *God* is used in this program, it respects the different knowing of each person.

Whatever understanding a man has, this program includes his perspective. It dictates none. This is a spiritual program, not a religious one. We often see our Higher Power was with us as a helpful force, long before we knew about it.

Today, I am grateful for God's care. May I learn to increase in trust and knowledge of God.

It is the greatest of all mistakes to do nothing because you can only do a little. Do what you can.

—*Sydney Smith*

We are capable of far more than we think. The task before us sometimes seems mountainous, but we don't have to do it all in one day. We can do only a little, although we want to accomplish the whole job at once. We must not let our desire for complete change all at once discourage us from doing what we can. We may need to look for a new job, or face the loneliness of ending a hurtful relationship, or hold firmly to our wisest fathering role with our children, or deal with an illness in ourselves or a loved one.

We do not have to face the tasks that challenge us by ourselves. We are all members of a large, quiet network of spiritual support for each other. We have our Twelve Step program, the loving strength of our Higher Power, and the companionship of other men and women in our group. With help, we can do what must be done. We only need to faithfully do a little at a time.

Today, I will remember that I am not alone. I have help in many forms, and I will do what I can.

Chaos demands to be recognized and experienced before letting itself be converted into a new order.

—Hermann Hesse

The forces of chaos and forces of order are always at work in the world. While many things are being built up, many are wearing down. It is a good thing, because life would be very boring in an unchanging state. But the chaos we met in our lives was often extreme and unusually destructive. We had to recognize it and feel the pain of it before we could build a new order. Looking back we can see that our First Step was just such an event.

All people have small chaotic events in their lives every day. If we take a moment and reflect on our present lives, we can certainly become aware of some ways in which things are in disarray. By simply letting ourselves know it in this moment, we get ready for the new order to begin.

I pray for courage and honesty to see the chaos which exists today. Help me become ready for the new order to evolve.

I have learned this: it is not what one does that is wrong, but what one becomes as a consequence of it.

—Oscar Wilde

There are countless ways to take shortcuts in life or to grab for pleasures. We could cheat on our income taxes, excuse a food binge, or lie to a loved one about where we've been. We say, "It won't hurt anyone!" "I wouldn't do it if it weren't for the other guy." Or, "Everyone does it." But if we are to like and respect ourselves, we need to live by the rules we believe in. Whether we get caught or not isn't the point. We cannot hold values and then repeatedly justify breaking them.

What does it do to us if we constantly fudge on our values? It undermines our self-esteem and damages the faith we have in ourselves. We do not expect to be perfect, but we must be accountable. If we are honest with ourselves, we admit our wrongs and reestablish our self-respect.

Today, I will take care to make choices that match my values.

Anyone who lives art knows that psychoanalysis has no monopoly on the power to heal. . . . Art and poetry have always been altering our ways of sensing and feeling—that is to say, altering the human body.

—Norman O. Brown

A man can lead a healing life on many levels. On one level, many of us have turned to healing professionals for help. That may strengthen our program and be very beneficial for many of our problems.

Relationships heal when they are loving, affirming, reliable, committed, and loyal. Nature heals: a tree, a walk through tall grass, a dry seedpod, or a potted plant gives life when we turn in its direction. Beauty heals: music, a poem, a novel, or a picture may move us to another plane and teach us about life. Meditation heals: solitude, quiet relaxation, prayer, and cosmic consciousness bring an inner peace. Laughter heals. Physical activity heals. Doing something for others helps us. At the basic level, accepting ourselves as lovable men, just as we are, is the foundation for all healing.

The forces for renewal and wholeness are varied. May I reach out to them and be healed by them.

Are you willing to be sponged out, erased,/ cancelled,/made nothing?/Are you willing to be made nothing?/dipped into oblivion?/If not, you will never really change.

—D. H. Lawrence

Many men have a self-centered attitude about change. They say, "Lift yourselves up by your boot-straps! Take charge! Be aggressive!" They have only a beginner's understanding of what real change is. When we try to change ourselves by our own methods, we simply give rebirth to our already limited controlling ideas. We recycle and intensify our problems.

This program has given us a profound possibility for change. We discover we are able to move beyond our compulsion to control by surrendering. The promises for recovery are clear and bright, if we yield to this program totally—but they do not come on our timetable. We yield. We allow ourselves to be helped. We allow change to overtake us. We earnestly seek to do our part. And change comes! It comes—not when we say, "Now I deserve it," but when we are ready to accept it.

Today, I surrender again. Each day I learn to surrender and grow deeper.

A person who is looking for something doesn't travel very fast.

— *E. B. White*

What do men really want? What are we seeking? Many of us have felt driven and still feel restless or compulsive at times. We frantically followed our impulses to self-destructive extremes. Even those painful actions of our past were motivated, at the bottom line, by a spiritual search. What did we really seek in the bottle, or in the passionate bed, or in our work? Slowing down enough every day to let ourselves know what we are looking for gives us a much better chance of finding it.

Today we can slow down by taking twenty minutes for solitude and quiet, for meditation or prayer. We can call a friend simply for a moment of contact. We might read something to give ourselves some ideas to ponder, or we can listen to music which will transport us to another world. Perhaps we can simply walk more slowly from our cars or the bus stop to our homes. Often it is not the events in our lives that bring change but the space between events.

Today, I will try to remember that slowing down may help me find what I am seeking.

*Just be what you are and speak from your guts
and heart—it's all a man has.*
                              —Hubert Humphrey

Some of us have doubted our inner voice so completely that we abandoned it totally. Many of us have discovered in recovery that by our denial we had violated our inner voice with lies, even to ourselves. Now we question whether we can trust our instincts, and we may not know what we feel.

Masculine spiritual recovery is a return to our guts and our heart. Standing up and speaking from our hearts may be difficult at times, but our self-respect rises as we do. That is where we go for our final decision making. We develop better reception for the inner voice as we live this program. We accept that we are never absolutely right. We continue with humility, knowing we may be wrong and listening to others and our Higher Power. Yet we must live with our choices.

I will seek the courage to be faithful to my own instincts.

A woman should be able to be both independent and dependent, active and passive, relaxed and serious, practical and romantic, tender and tough minded, thinking and feeling, dominant and submissive. So, obviously, should a man!
—Pierre Mornell

The weakest men, most vulnerable to stresses in life, are those with narrow ideas about masculinity. In our growth, we are finding parts of ourselves we didn't know were there. Some of us are finding the tough part of us that makes it possible to stand up to our bosses or our wives or lovers when necessary. We are also finding the soft parts, warm parts, sad parts. And the greater the variety of sides we develop, the more successful we are in meeting life.

Whatever we discover about ourselves is another example of being human. Sometimes we might think what we feel is not right, or is weak or sick. We need never fear our feelings. The denial of our feelings had devastating effects on us. Knowing and accepting our many sides will lead us into strength and health.

I am thankful that I am able to be both sides of many coins.

It is extraordinary how extraordinary the ordinary person is.

—*George F. Will*

At our meetings, we often hear stories of the courage of ordinary people and their triumph against great odds. When we hear of a person's life being restored, we are witnesses to miracles. Our friends are heroes and so are we. As a man describes his passage from insanity to recovery, we are moved. Whenever we are truly open to knowing the people around us, whether at a meeting or in getting to know a neighbor, we will see heroism. It is amazing that when we get to know most people, and hear what their lives have been like, we find so much to admire and respect. It is a privilege to have such friends. It is amazing that they are so abundant when we open ourselves to them. God truly does speak to us through others.

I am grateful when I think about the extraordinary people around me and the courage in each of them. I am grateful to be among them.

Free man is by necessity insecure; thinking man by necessity uncertain.

—Erich Fromm

We hear comments like, "Hang in there!" "Don't quit now," "Don't give up the ship!" When our outlook is gloomy and pessimistic, we should remember we are not in charge and we are not all-knowing. We cannot predict what will be around the next corner. If a difficult problem looms before us, we cannot be sure what help might also be there for us to meet the problem.

Our compulsion for control tempts us to quit and give ourselves over to defeat. Then the outcome would be settled and predictable. We no longer would have to live with the insecurity of not knowing the future. When we are tempted to indulge in our addictive ways, or to return to a relationship that isn't good for us, or to face a painful problem, it helps to recall that change is a basic fact of life. However stressful this moment is, it will change. Not at our command, but it will change. We aren't in control of outcomes, but we can choose now to "hang in there" and to give our energy only toward positive solutions.

May I have the serenity to accept the process and the courage to be true to my part. Outcomes I will leave for the future.

Some of us, observing that ideals are rarely achieved, proceed to the error of considering them worthless. Such an error is greatly harmful. True North cannot be reached either, since it is an abstraction, but it is of enormous importance, as all the world's travelers can attest.

—*Steve Allen*

How many of us, seeing others who failed to live fully by their ideals, cried, "Hypocrite!" Perhaps we even pointed to others' shortcomings to excuse our own. Now, in this program, we may be tempted to swing like a pendulum to the other extreme. We may hold to our values and principles so tightly that we are perfectionistic.

The idea that True North cannot ever be reached is very useful. If we don't achieve True North, even though we establish it as our standard, we will generally be heading in the right direction. Although we never perfectly achieve our ideals, they remain our standards today for orienting our lives.

I do accept standards for my life. I will not beat on myself for my imperfections.

I wasn't exactly brought up in one of those Norman Rockwell paintings you used to see on the cover of the Saturday Evening Post.
— *Reggie Jackson*

We have many myths about other people's lives. When we compare ourselves to these stories, we come up short. We have the TV families of *Father Knows Best* or *The Waltons* in our minds. We may have stories our father told about his moment of glory and how he met his challenges. Any of these images selects part of the truth and highlights it, creating a myth that might be worthwhile if we don't take it too literally.

Living real life never feels as serene as our fantasies. A myth lifts us up, carries us away to other possibilities, but we should always take it with a grain of salt. A father's recollections or a Norman Rockwell painting romanticizes a piece of reality by omitting the drudgery and confusion of life. Myths are meant as inspirations, not as measurements of our lives.

The difficulties and confusion I feel may just be part of real life. Serenity comes when I accept the mixture that real life is.

The first skill needed for the Inner Game is called "letting it happen." This means gradually building a trust in the innate ability of your body to learn and to perform.
　　　　　　　　　　　　—W. Timothy Gallwey

A strange and intriguing mystery confronts us in the Twelve Steps. We are mending our ways; we are becoming accountable; we are striving to do what is right, yet we are learning to let go. This seems like a contradiction of logic, but it leads us to a spiritual awakening.

We are becoming like the accomplished tennis player who has practiced diligently to develop every detail of his skill. Yet when he is playing the game, he cannot focus on control. He must get his ego out of the way and let himself go. It is in letting go that he rises to his highest level of fulfillment. Today we will do what we must. We can make the choices we are faced with. Then we allow ourselves to be carried along by our Higher Power to complete and fulfill the process.

I will look for opportunities to let it happen today.

The first springs of great events, like those of great rivers, are often mean and little.
— *Jonathan Swift*

Our lives are like streams which flow through time. Looking at the flow of our whole lives, we see the interconnections of many days that seemed minor. Each day contributes to the stream of goals and faith and relationships. As we look at the flow of a whole river, we see at its beginning a little trickle of water here, joining another trickle there, slowly gathering together a stream that develops force and direction.

We may look for intensity in our lives and ignore the quiet. Much of our lives may have been lived on a roller coaster of major crises. As terrible as it seemed, it was not dull. Today may seem rather boring. But in recovery we learn to appreciate the more subtle trickle that a good day can be. Simply continuing with the flow—of our program, of faithfulness to our values, of being emotionally present in our relationships—adds up to a rich life.

May I see the continuity of my life in the simple moments of this day.

*Friendship with oneself is all-important, because
without it one cannot be friends with anyone else
in the world.*

—*Eleanor Roosevelt*

In recovery, perhaps first we make peace with ourselves, and not until later do we become our own friends. We have been at war with ourselves and in turmoil with our families, even while feeling like victims. This program lays out Twelve Steps we can follow to become friends with ourselves. In recovery we may still feel self-hate when we constantly monitor our every action, when we react to our mistakes by berating ourselves, and when we dwell on past offenses. Would we put a friend through that?

A true friend will accept you as you are. He doesn't put you down or call you derogatory names. He'll give you honest feedback and won't put on a false front. He'll support you when you're in trouble. Being our own friend means doing these things for ourselves. Perhaps we can even embrace and be kind to the part of ourselves that is addicted and codependent.

---

*Today, I will be a friend to my whole self—even the parts
of me I have rejected.*

I shall tell you a great secret, my friend. Do not wait for the last judgment. It takes place every day.

—*Albert Camus*

We live our program in one-day portions—and our actions today have immediate consequences. For instance, if we listen to a brother or a sister in the program, we may be enriched and the other person strengthened for today's challenge. We don't have to confront every temptation of life on this day—only the portion we can handle. Our old insanity would have us predict the entire story of our future from today's limited viewpoint. But our spiritual orientation guides us to restrain ourselves. We simply live in this moment.

The rewards of recovery are granted every day. We begin with the gift of a new day and new possibilities. We now have relationships that sustain us through difficulty and give us reason to celebrate. We have a new feeling of self-respect and hope.

I am grateful for the rewards of each day in my spiritual awakening.

The natural world is a spiritual house. . . . Man walks there through forests of physical things that are also spiritual things, that watch him with affectionate looks.

—*Charles Baudelaire*

As we live this program, we learn to see the spiritual in physical things. Whatever we see or hear, whatever happens in our lives may carry a spiritual message. Some of us will say, "God is telling me something." Others, whose understanding of God takes another form, will say, "There is a spiritual message in this if I can read it."

But many men, having had relationships that were abusive and painful, find it hard to imagine the spirit of things watching them with affection, and not hostility. Many of us have been used, and we have used others. We don't expect affectionate relationships, but could it be that the spiritual world loves us and we don't know it? Perhaps if we think about this for a while, we also will become more loving.

The generosity of God is expressed in all kinds of physical things. I will remember that the spiritual is affectionate toward me.

I drink not from mere joy in wine nor to scoff at faith—no, only to forget myself for a moment, that only do I want of intoxication, that alone.
—Omar Khayyam

What has been our drug of choice? It may be alcohol. It may be sugar or gambling or dependent relationships. Some men have used anger, sex, sports, or the accumulation of money. Growing in this program, we learn there is a great brotherhood among us. Our problems have not been only with a certain substance or a given behavior. We have been seduced and trapped by a ritual of forgetting ourselves. If we hadn't found one way, we may have found another. In giving one up, we often found ourselves drawn to a new substitute.

Now we are learning to accept ourselves and to forget ourselves in healthier ways. We all need to move beyond the bounds of an oppressive ego. In our old style, we could not learn healthy releases because we were hooked on unhealthy ones. Now we are learning meditation, making friends, helping others, and letting go as ways to forget ourselves.

I pray for help today in staying away from self-destructive intoxications so I am able to learn healthy releases.

*Fine friendship requires duration rather than
fitful intensity.*

—Aristotle

Once we have embarked upon this program, we
find spiritual recovery through relationships more
than any other single factor. We find it through relationships with other people, with ourselves, and with
our Higher Power. But most men in recovery need to
learn how to be in a relationship. We have to give up
ideas that a friendship is an intense connection or a
conflict-free blending of like minds.

A meaningful friendship is a long-term dialogue. If
there is conflict or if we make a mistake or fail to do
what our friend wants of us, we don't end the friendship. We simply have the next exchange to resolve the
differences. Our dialogue continues over time, and
time—along with many amends—builds the bond.
With it develops a deepening sense of reliability and
trusting one another. When we have lived with our
friend through many experiences—or with our Higher
Power—we gain a feeling that we really know him or
her in a way we could never have in a brief intense
connection.

---

*Today, I will do what I need to do to be reliable in my
friendships.*

Indeed, this need of individuals to be right is so great that they are willing to sacrifice themselves, their relationships, and even love for it.
—*Reuel Howe*

We may have an inner drive to be right—and even to prove we are right. We often have been expected to know about the world and how things work, as if our manhood were tied to knowing. So when we don't know the right answer, or when a person disagrees with us, we may get upset because we feel our masculine honor is in question.

We should always remember that our honor requires being honest, not being right. Our masculinity is being true to ourselves as men, not being invincible. Demanding that our opinions always be accepted as right is destructive to our relationships. It cuts us off from people we love, and becomes hostile and selfish. We are learning to allow room for differences; we can love and respect people we disagree with. And we all have a right to be wrong part of the time.

I don't have to have all the right answers. Today, my ideas are just one man's honest thoughts.

I've never started a fight, but I never pulled back from a fight either.

—Billy Martin

Sometimes we walk around with chips on our shoulders. We're like a tightly wound spring ready to jump at the slightest trigger, when other times we would let the same event go unnoticed. We even say self-righteously, "I didn't start it." Now that we are becoming more responsible for ourselves, we are owning our part in relationships. Maybe we have a problem with being like a spring ready to jump. When we are like that, we are difficult to live with or be around.

We can change by getting in touch with our pain. We need to explore our feelings. Perhaps we need to be honest with ourselves about low self-esteem, about feelings of loneliness or fear. Then we must talk with another person or our group about our feelings and continue to talk about them. In this way we become reconciled to ourselves and to our friends around us.

―――――――

God, help me accept my own pain, and help me be tolerant of my friends' mistakes.

A life of reaction is a life of slavery, intellectually and spiritually. One must fight for a life of action not reaction.

—Rita Mae Brown

All men in recovery confront their reactive habits in relationships. Whether we came to recovery as a codependent or as an addict, we soon must face how much other people's behavior has been a cue for our own reactions. There is always a three-part process in any reaction—first, the other person's behavior; second, a moment of choosing a response; and third, our reaction. But in our spiritual slavery, we don't notice the choice stage. It feels automatic. It may feel as though *the other person made me do it.*

No amount of changing on someone else's part can change us. We are becoming more responsible for our own lives and for our own behavior regardless of others around us. There is liberation in noticing the choice stage. It is tough to follow through on our choices, but when we do, it is truly a sign of a grown man. Then a remarkable thing happens—our self-esteem rises.

Today, I will pause to notice the choices I have in the moment between someone's action and my reaction.

MAY

Gardening is an active participation in the deepest mysteries of the universe.
—*Thomas Berry*

We grow in our spirituality by participating in activities that convey a sense of awe and mystery. Tending growing plants does this for some of us. Playing and listening to music, appreciating and creating art and literature do it for others. Hiking in the wilderness, camping, fishing, hunting, or photography have the same value. Membership in a religious group and attending services are other important ways. Engaging in the loving feelings in relationships does this for many of us.

As men in recovery, we need active ways to move beyond the boundaries of our own skins. We need to know we are part of a larger whole which has mysteries we cannot fully solve. When we identify our own ways of being spiritual, we can give them more respect. Perhaps we can also explore some other ways we have not developed.

Today, I will participate in the mysteries and beauties of life.

Do not reveal your thoughts to everyone, lest you drive away your good luck.
—Apocrypha, Ecclesiasticus 8:19

We've had problems in our lives with limits. We have done some things to excess and others we have endlessly postponed. Sometimes we haven't had good judgment about what we ought to tell someone or whom we ought to tell. We may have kept secrets that made us lonely and sick. Other times we exposed too much in inappropriate situations and hurt someone else or ourselves. Developing these internal limits is a quiet change that comes with recovery. Gradually, we gain a stronger feeling of self-respect and become more intuitive about when to express something and when not to.

Secrets are links in our chains of bondage to isolation, addiction, and codependency. Yet, when we are compelled to tell everything, we lack the feeling of self-containment that comes from maturity. We need a sense of privacy which is the freedom to choose what and when to confide in a friend. What does our intuition tell us today about our privacy and our openness?

Today, I will listen to my inner messages about what I need to discuss with others and when I need to withhold.

"Honesty" without compassion and under-
standing is not honest, but subtle hostility.
                                    —*Rose N. Franzblau*

Any good thing can be used in hurtful or destructive ways. Our entire recovery is based on a funda-
mental premise of honesty. But our honesty becomes
distorted and hurtful when we are not in tune with
our motivations. A man who contradicts other group
members to feel superior rather than to be helpful is
being hostile. If we criticize people about things they
cannot change, we are only hurting them. In making
amends, we should not approach people who are better off without our contact, or who are better off without our confessions.

As we grow, we encounter more parts of ourselves
that may be hurtful. We need to accept those parts
too, not condemn ourselves for being human, not
hide our destructive impulses from ourselves. Then
our honesty with ourselves and with others will not be
tainted by dishonest motives.

I pray for honesty with myself first so my honesty with
others will be pure.

*What if the interests of the self were expanded to
... a God's eye view of the human scene ...
accepting failure as being as natural an
occurrence as success in the stupendous human
drama ... as little cause for worry and concern
as having to play the role of a loser in a summer
theater performance.*

—Huston Smith

Detachment is a mature and wise way of dealing
with life experiences. It is sometimes difficult because
it challenges our maturity. How can we take failure
lightly when we have been taught all our lives to be
winners and to accept every dare? How can we stand
back from a loved one who is anxious and in pain, still
be supportive, but not take charge as if it were our
problem?

We can question some of our old ideas. Maybe we
were wrong to think we should always be Prince
Charming who rescues maidens in distress. Maybe our
ideas about being winners have been compulsions
that stood in our way of having true friends.

———

*As my perspective is changed, I will get stronger in
maintaining a healthy detachment.*

Living itself, [is] a task of such immediacy, variety, beauty, and excitement that one is powerless to resist its wild embrace.
—E. B. White

Our First Step in this program introduces us to a radical idea—that accepting our powerlessness is beneficial. Yielding to life's embrace takes us in wonderful directions. The experience of meeting this still-unformed day, defining how we will live today, making contact with our Higher Power, accepting the variety and the beauty that is here for us—far exceeds our individual power. Yet in surrendering to life as it unfolds, we find ourselves on an adventure. This is like reading a good story or unraveling an exciting mystery.

Anyone, whether he has our affliction or not, who tries to take control of what cannot be controlled, brings trouble to himself. Today let us engage with life.

I will accept both the embrace and the insecurity of not being in charge.

Little importance has been given to body awareness. The emphasis is on achievement rather than awareness. Yet it is only those athletes who have a highly developed kinesthetic sense—muscle sense—who ever achieve high levels of excellence.

—W. Timothy Gallwey

The outstanding athlete is guided by the feeling in his muscles and bones. He knows as he moves how much force to apply, how to place the ball on target, or how to dive gracefully. Competitiveness and achievement are useful in our lives. Winning provides us with motivation and fun. But when we give primary importance to being a winner, we weaken and lose balance.

Our balance is strengthened through more awareness in all aspects of our lives. If a ruler refused to hear news from a certain section of his country, his leadership would suffer. When we ignore our feelings and don't reflect on our daily lives, we become weaker and less adequate men. As we read this page today, we are opening ourselves to internal messages and opening the windows of awareness.

God, help me find more balance and learn to be more aware.

The newest computer can merely compound, at speed, the oldest problem in relations between human beings, and in the end the communicator will be confronted with the old problem, of what to say and how to say it.
—*Edward R. Murrow*

We may reduce our difficulties with others to communication problems, yet the remedy may remain unclear. How can we become more responsible for our share of the communication? Can we stop blaming others? When we improve in those ways, our relationships get better.

Clear, specific, and direct language will help us be more responsible and less blaming. We can use simple words that expose the truth rather than words that hide or sugarcoat it. We can use specific examples and give details rather than generalities or hints. We can be more direct by using *you* and *me* language. In the process, we yield to the truth within ourselves—and become more honest.

Today, I will be aware of communicating clearly, specifically, and directly.

Children begin by loving their parents; as they grow older they judge them; sometimes they forgive them.

—Oscar Wilde

The mature man eventually forgives his parents. Any adult can look back and see childhood wrongs and unfairness. Many of us were disappointed by our parents, even neglected or hurt by them. We certainly didn't get all we wanted or needed. Yet, upon joining the ranks of grown men and women, we become responsible for ourselves. Every situation has limited choices, and we work with what we've got. As adults, we realize this is exactly where our parents were when we were children. They, too, were born into an imperfect world and had to do the best they could.

When we can forgive our parents, we are free to accept them as they are, as we might a friend. We can accept them, enjoy the relationship, and forget about collecting old debts. Making peace with them imparts to us the strengths of previous generations and helps us be more at peace with ourselves.

I pray for the maturity and the wisdom to be more forgiving of my parents.

I learned from them that inspiration does not come like a bolt, nor is it kinetic, energetic striving, but it comes into us slowly and quietly and all the time, though we must regularly and every day give it a little chance to start flowing, prime it with a little solitude and idleness.
—Brenda Ueland

We tend to be action-oriented and concerned about showing results in the shortest period of time. Our world has emphasized this outlook, especially for men. Now we are seeking spiritual progress. We are on a journey seeking a relationship with our Higher Power, with ourselves, and with others.

Spiritual progress is made by pushing aside busyness and efficiency. We become receptive to inspiration by allowing empty spaces in our lives, some solitude and idleness. This moment—right now—is one such time. It is not clearly goal-oriented. Rather it is a moment when we reflect on ourselves as recovering men. We become receptive to inspiration, to a deeper wisdom, to that part of life which we do not command.

I will remember today that spiritual progress comes only when I make room for it in my life.

"You are accepted!" . . . accepted by that which is greater than you and the name of which you do not know. Do not ask the name now, perhaps you will know it later. Do not try to do anything, perhaps later you will do much. Do not seek for anything, do not perform anything, do not intend anything. Simply accept the fact you are accepted.

—Paul Tillich

New possibilities opened up when we accepted our powerlessness. These possibilities came to us from beyond ourselves. We can open ourselves to acceptance by being responsible for ourselves and practicing the Twelve Steps. We can't improve upon the message that we are accepted, nor can we nail it down. In fact, the very moment we try to impose our control over it, it begins to evaporate.

We can receive this message of acceptance only when we are humble and open to it. After learning to surrender in the First Step of this program, we are ready to yield to messages of acceptance.

I am grateful for the acceptance which has come my way.

There is no shortcut to life. To the end of our days, life is a lesson imperfectly learned.
— *Harrison E. Salisbury*

There are no perfect days. We have struggled hard against this truth. In our demanding ways, we haven't wanted life to be a process; we have wanted to reach a secure point of arrival. We have struggled against the dialogue and learning process of experience. We've looked for a "fix" and for perfection. Even now in recovery we long to "get it right." We continue to learn and to grow, but the lessons we learn are not the things we expected. We grieve the lateness of our learning, and then we go on to learn more.

As we grow in this program, we learn how to learn. We become more accepting of life as a process with no shortcut to the truth. We learn to engage in the process and accept that there usually is no right or wrong answer at the end of our search.

Today, may I accept the truth which comes from the lessons of my experience—and be tolerant of its incompleteness.

In my friend, I find a second self.
                                    —Isabel Norton

Our mates and close friends present us with another view on what it is to be a human being. In being close we lower our barriers and get a feeling for what life is like from that person's perspective. We develop a feeling of empathy for him or her, and we multiply our life experiences by participating with others.

Through our closeness to someone, we might be confronted by a new awareness of ourselves. We may see something about ourselves we don't like and could never have seen on our own. We may see how similar we are to our friends, or how different, or how common and human our problems are. While each man lives his own life, through empathy we are given another window on the experience of living. Having a friend is a rich experience which increases our wisdom about life.

I am thankful for relationships. I feel grateful that I am not alone.

*As long as you keep a person down, some part of
you has to be down there to hold him down, so it
means you cannot soar as you otherwise might.*
—Marion Anderson

Because of our resentments we sometimes get tense.
We say we aren't going to have contact with our parents until they do something we expect of them. Or
we hold out on a friend because we want an apology
for an injury or injustice.

Sadly, we become more tense, more limited in our
own joy, by holding someone else to our expectations.
Our lives can be much richer and more fulfilled when
we let go of these expectations. We can let go of manipulating or drawing forth the responses we want.
Our manipulations and pouting make life too boring
and limited. No one else need stand in the way of our
pleasure of being adult men.

*Today, I will let go of my claims on others so I can be free
to soar.*

Often the wisdom of the body clarifies the despair of the spirit.
—Marion Woodman

The unity of body and spirit becomes more real for us as we learn to listen to the messages our bodies give. Perhaps if we are frequently ill with a cold we are hiding from the fact that we are discouraged and in need of something for our spirit. We all face the problems at times of sleeplessness or backaches or allergies. These are not moral problems but problems that go with being human. When we are open to the spirit dimension, we look for the part that may express a message from our spiritual selves.

As we notice our physical selves today, we perhaps feel a tension in a muscle or a sensation somewhere that can speak to us about our deeper feelings. The message may not be clear at first. Spiritual messages are not quick answers, but if we listen to our questions a while, the answers may gradually become clear. Simply being open to the messages strengthens us for our tasks and deepens our spiritual self-awareness.

Today, I am learning to listen to the wisdom of my own body.

If you can't fight and you can't flee, flow.
—*Robert Eliot*

Too often, we men have lived with a single answer to every situation: win. We saw our friendships in competitive terms, so we couldn't let our guard down. We looked at life as a challenge to be conquered rather than something to be enjoyed. Therefore, our first impulse was to fight and come out a winner. Many of us have played life like a game with only winners and losers, and we have neglected the deeper meaning in our experiences. Living that way, many of us have felt like losers.

We all experience moments when a situation is much more powerful than we are. Those moments feel like defeat unless we allow them to open a whole new viewpoint on our lives. When we can flow with a situation, which will have its own way anyhow, we have become more mature men. We can breathe a sigh of relief because much of the tension in our lives is reduced when we stop trying to conquer every moment and instead simply flow with it.

Today, I will practice playing a new game of flowing and thereby deepen my awareness of life.

The work will teach you how to do it.
                                    —Estonian proverb

We learn this spiritual program as we learned to ride a bike or to swim. We could never get it from reading a book. We only learn it by doing it and by following the example of others. As we first entered the program, we may have thought, "Oh I understand this. In twelve meetings I'll have it licked."

Many men have had difficulty trusting, so we try to understand everything before we get involved in it. But as long as we try to figure it out first, we remain on the outside looking in. Doing the practical things in this program—taking inventories and making amends, praying for guidance from our Higher Power, carrying the message to others, selecting a sponsor—will teach us the essentials for spiritual recovery.

Today, I will take the risk of learning by living the spiritual life.

What sort of God would it be who only pushed from without?

—Goethe

Oh, we hate to be pushed! We get upset and angry when someone is pushing on us. What man likes it? Sometimes God does pushing, and it takes a while for us to realize it is God's pressure on us that we feel. Our natural reaction is to resist and push back.

When we keep getting headaches or stomachaches, maybe we should listen for the message. An unsettled feeling in our lives—about women, money, health, work, or something else—may carry a message for us. God might be pushing from within. In this program we try to develop our ability to hear God's will for us. Sometimes a problem is, in fact, a spiritual message. When we stop resisting and start listening, we soon grow wiser and stronger.

God, your message is not always clear to me. Today, I will try to put aside my own habit of pushing back so I can have a clearer mind to receive it.

*One should learn to enjoy the neighbor's garden,
however small; the roses straggling over the
fence, the scent of lilacs drifting across the road.*
—Henry Van Dyke

There are many gifts around us which we overlook
when we're busy dealing with our anxieties and obli-
gations. We talk about burning out from our high-
intensity lifestyles. We act as though nothing would
get done if we didn't do it ourselves. We get so en-
grossed in fighting with the frustrations of life that we
fail to see the good things coming our way that took
no effort on our part.

As we look around us this very moment, what good
things do we find? Has a friend given a warm hello? Is
the sun shining? The rain falling? Has the traffic
flowed smoothly? We have no claim on these generous events, and we can't say God smiles on us when
we have them or He frowns when we don't. We can
say there are always generous forces coming our way
which comfort and heal us. We only need to take time
to enjoy them.

---

*Today, I will take some quiet moments to notice the good
things coming my way. I will be grateful for them.*

The world is full of people looking for spectacular happiness while they snub contentment.

—*Doug Larson*

We are men on a quest. We seek the serenity of being friendly toward the world and toward ourselves. The spiritual practices we follow are personal and quiet, not spectacular or dazzling. We have been part of the throng seeking stimulating highs. Some of us know the excitement and escape of saving others from their own troubles or drowning ourselves in activity and work. We may know the mellowness of a drug or food binge. Perhaps we know the heart-pounding intensity of shoplifting, gambling, or sexual pursuit.

The way of life suggested by this simple program changes us deeply if we fully surrender to it. This spiritual quest changes us slowly over time, and our reward is contentment. It produces a joy, a feeling of well-being, which is far richer than the momentary pleasures we sought in the past.

Today, I am grateful for a way of life which leads me toward a contentment I can rely on.

Truth is a demure lady, much too ladylike to knock you on the head and drag you to her cave. She is there, but the people must want her and seek her out.

—*William F. Buckley, Jr.*

As we develop a deeper and more reliable friendship with ourselves, we have little hunches or inner blips of feeling that tell us private truths. Ancient scriptures called it "a still, small voice." We usually sense this inner message somewhere in our body. Some men say it's in the heart, others say in the gut, or ear, or on their shoulders. When we are too focused on what others think and feel and what the world says is truth, we don't notice our inner voice; it doesn't get much chance to develop. It never hits us over the head; it requires silence and respect to be heard.

As we follow the Steps, we learn to regularly visit the cave of this demure lady, Truth, and seek out her wisdom. The more we listen and the more we respect the truths we receive in our quietness, the more wisdom we are given.

I will listen to the personal wisdom whispered by that still, small voice within.

Everyone is a bore to someone. That is unimportant. The thing to avoid is being a bore to oneself.

—*Gerald Brenan*

As teenagers most of us were very self-conscious and concerned about how we looked to others. That was a normal stage in development. But, for many of us, our addictions began at that age, or the addictions of others affected us. Our emotional development stopped. We didn't develop an inner reference point, a relationship with our Higher Power that influenced us and helped us weigh other people's opinions.

In recovery, we resumed our emotional and spiritual development where it had stopped. It is liberating to know that how we feel about something is important. We can follow our interests and pursue our commitments. We need not be ruled by others' feelings. With our regular pattern of taking our inventory, praying, and meditating, we are developing a relationship with ourselves which builds character and maturity.

Today, I will give importance to how I feel, what I believe, and what is interesting to me.

If you do not express your own original ideas, if you do not listen to your own being, you will have betrayed yourself.

—Rollo May

Those of us who go around trying to be right and do everything right are likely to betray ourselves. We stifle our impulses and control our intuition because we can't be certain that we are correct. As a spiritual exercise, we could stop now and listen to our inner selves and state our own ideas. What comes out may break the illusion of perfection and free us to proceed with life.

We all have original ideas if we just notice them. What images come to mind while listening to music? What do our dreams tell us? New insights sometimes come by physical activity. Conversation with a friend can help lead us to our wisdom. Our growing strength as recovering men requires that we listen to our own messages and then take some risks to express them.

Today, I will take risks by stating my ideas. I will stand up for myself by listening to my intuition.

*You see, I just can't stop! Or tie myself to any
one. I have affairs that last as long as a year, a
year and a half, months and months of love,
both tender and voluptuous, but in the end—it is
as inevitable as death—time marches on and
lust peters out.*

—*Philip Roth*

Fears of intimacy, of learning about ourselves in a
committed relationship, have kept many of us lonely.
Focusing on the need for a sexual high helps us avoid
the intimacy we fear. Whether we are in a long-term
relationship or not, thinking that sex is love limits our
chances for a comfortable intimacy. Sex is an expression of an intimacy that already exists, rather than a
way to become intimate.

Many of us fear closeness beyond the romantic
stage. Others of us have pursued closeness, but when
we met our own emptiness we said that wasn't the
right person for us and ran in search of another excitement. The problem for us isn't the choice between singleness and marriage, but between letting someone
truly know us or not.

*I will set aside my fears and learn the pleasure of
intimacy.*

Edith Bunker: *I was just thinking. In all the years we been married, you never once said you was sorry.*
Archie Bunker: *Edith, I'll gladly say that I'm sorry—if I ever do anything wrong.*
—*Norman Lear*

We can laugh at Archie because we see a part of ourselves in him. We have lived in a cloud of denial, blind to our faults. If we weren't actually blind to them, perhaps we just refused to admit them because we did not dare. Changing this pattern takes time and determination. We make progress in recovery when we stop focusing on what is wrong with others and start being accountable for ourselves. We grow when we are willing to amend our lives and accept forgiveness for our mistakes.

A feeling of self-respect flows into us when we stand up and say "I did something wrong." This statement also says, "I have the strength to face my responsibilities and repair my mistakes." It is surprisingly helpful to our self-esteem, and it improves our relationships.

Today, I will be accountable for my actions and will admit my mistakes.

For him who confesses, shams are over and realities have begun; he has exteriorized his rottenness. If he has not actually got rid of it, he at least no longer smears it over with a hypocritical show of virtue.

—William James

On the path we are following, confession is a frequent part of our experience. We admit our powerlessness; we make a searching and fearless moral inventory of ourselves and admit our wrongs; we make amends to people we have harmed; and we continue with personal inventory, promptly admitting our wrongs. With each of these Steps we grow spiritually. By expressing on the outside what we privately know inside, we feel relief and gain self-respect.

Sometimes we have harbored and protected a real rottenness inside that needed to be exposed so we could change. Other times, what we felt was rottenness turned out—under the light of confession—to be only a human foible in need of airing. In either case, we grew stronger as we drew closer to reality and gave up the show of virtue by admitting our mistakes.

I will walk the path of recovery today by confessing my wrongs promptly.

A rock pile ceases to be a rock pile the moment a single man contemplates it, bearing within him the image of a cathedral.
—*Antoine de Saint-Exupery*

Images cost nothing and can be so enriching. Every man has some form of rock pile in his life. One has a problem within a relationship, another is burdened with the daily routine of living, someone else has a perplexing job, and another has too much time on his hands.

We can open ourselves to images of what might be. Let us dream of other possibilities. We know it takes many years to build a cathedral, but each cathedral began as an image in someone's mind. What would we like to grow toward in our relationships? What can we do within ourselves today to carry us in that direction? Do we envision ourselves as successful in our work? What small steps will carry us toward the visions we cherish?

Today, I am grateful for my imagination. I will be open to having faith in possibilities.

At times almost all of us envy the animals. They suffer and die, but do not seem to make a "problem" of it.

—Alan Watts

When we sit quietly and open ourselves to contact with our Higher Power, problems may come to mind. We seek some wisdom beyond ourselves to help us meet the challenges of this day. For many of us men, the greatest problem is our thinking rather than the situations we have to deal with.

Unlike animals, we complicate what is very simple. The pain we face is never fair, so we need not waste time trying to understand the justice or injustice of it. Our problems may seem large or overwhelming from today's perspective. By tomorrow or next month most of them will be resolved in some way, and we may not even remember them. Our spiritual path teaches us to do first things first each day and not fret about the outcome. We turn outcomes over to the will of God.

Today, I will use the simplicity of the animals as my guide.

I sidestep the either/or choices of logic and choose both.

—Ken Feit

Men like us have often had a lifestyle guided by either/or logic. We think we must either conquer the challenge we see before us or we will be failures. We think loved ones must either meet our needs or they do not love us. We think we must either be perfect or we are unacceptable.

Let us now step back from the rigidity of such unhealthy logic. Much of human experience and many answers to our problems don't come in neatly tied packages. As we learn to think and feel in more flexible ways, we find life gets better. Using our intuition at times, rather than always following rigid rules for life, improves the recipe. The arrogance of our thought process has sometimes told us we had the answer, but it closed us to the growth which only comes by trusting our feelings. If we make mistakes, we can learn from them and go on. Many of the most ingenious inventions came not by rigidly following rules, but by following an inner feeling.

Today, I will be open to more possibilities in my thinking.

We cannot approach prayer as we do everything else in our push-button, instant society. There are no prayer pills or enlightenment capsules.
—*Janie Gustafson*

Prayer is the relationship between each man and his Higher Power. Our approach to this relationship is guided by our understanding of God. How other men and women have prayed and related to God throughout history may guide us today.

Any relationship is a process, not a momentary event with an instantaneous outcome. It builds with repeated contact and dialogue. With give and take, prayer is our honesty encountering God and our openness hearing God expressed on God's terms. Like any relationship, prayer includes all our feelings—anger, fear, and mistrust, as well as generosity, goodwill, and gratitude. Gradually, we see the events of our lives through the wisdom and detachment our spiritual relationship provides.

I return now to my dialogue with God, asking only for knowledge of God's will and the power to carry it out.

A frontier is never a place; it is a time and a way of life. Frontiers pass, but they endure in their people.

—Hal Borland

Frontiers are borders, and in our development we meet them again and again. Our first loves as teenagers were emotional and spiritual frontiers. Leaving home after childhood was another. Becoming a father, perhaps another. Some frontiers are very generous and exciting, while others are frightening, dangerous. Certainly this program has been a frontier for us.

To stay alive spiritually we need to continually go to the borders of our experience—or go back and face an old one from a new angle. We may encounter a new border in learning God's will for us in a new way, or in learning a new handicraft or sport, or meeting a life experience we didn't expect. We accumulate these memories within us. Some frontiers from long ago exist within us as if they were just yesterday. What frontiers stand out in our lives as we look back? What spiritual learning came from them? This is how we grow as men.

I am grateful for past frontiers that endure within me. They have strengthened and deepened my manhood.

Compassion is the ultimate and most meaningful embodiment of emotional maturity. It is through compassion that a person achieves the highest peak and deepest reach in his or her search for self-fulfillment.

—Arthur Jersild

Being compassionate is similar to what we call support in this program. We get outside our own self-centered egos and care about someone beyond ourselves. In the process we are helped and changed —perhaps more than the person we are helping.

As we mature, we learn that not all help is beneficial. It is more helpful to confront a friend in his delusion than to accept his misguided actions. Such tough honesty supports his strength and his ability to work the Steps. Sometimes it is hard to be a friend to a man in great pain. We might prefer to pull away rather than be with him as he suffers, but we can be more compassionate if we accept our powerlessness to cure his pain. Compassion has a reverberating effect in relationships. Not only do we give it and grow from the experience, we also become the receivers of what we send out.

Today, I will practice compassion in my relationships.

JUNE

In music, in the sea, in a flower, in a leaf, in an act of kindness . . . I see what people call God in all these things.

— Pablo Casals

The Third Step refers to "God as we understood Him." The pathways to meeting our Higher Power and to our spiritual awakening are all around. Every tree and every leaf on every tree, as it rustles in the wind, expresses God in our lives. When the little bird flies overhead or when it comes to visit the feeder, we are being visited by a spirit. When the sky boils with a storm, when lightning and thunder crash, we are witness to power greater than ourselves with a history beyond the centuries. The beautiful works of art created by our fellow human travelers on this journey through life are expressions of their courage to reach out and create something. A line of music moves us and we feel the spirit.

A child makes a drawing and gives it away. A neighbor helps you start your car. You treat the clerk at the checkout counter like a real person. Whatever word we use for God, if we decide to be open and receptive, we find God in the little details of our lives. Spiritual awakening is a wonderful daily occurrence.

God, open my senses to take in your presence more fully.

Remember! You're two different animals. Men and women cannot totally unite.
—Pierre Mornell

As we relate to women, we are often driven by needs, which no person could meet, and hampered by ignorance of what the opposite sex is really like. Perhaps we want to lose ourselves in a romantic closeness as we once lost ourselves in addiction and codependency. Then we get hurt and angry when the impossible doesn't happen. Or we fail to understand that one woman's reactions are different from our own.

The dialogue between the sexes is as old as the generations. It will always be a mixture of fascination, mystery, frustration, and new understandings. When we realize we cannot merge with a woman, take her over, or be taken over by her, we will meet her as a separate person, and our relationships will become vastly more peaceful.

Thanks to God for the differences. Let me learn more about them and accept them.

Almost anything you do will be insignificant, but it is very important that you do it.
—Mohandas Gandhi

Looking back at yesterday, looking at today, what sense do we have of progress in our growth? Probably nothing very significant. Sometimes it is amazing how little a person can accomplish in a day's efforts. Yet, what alternative do we have? Only that we could do nothing. Or worse, we could return to our old ways.

Gandhi, one of the greatest spiritual leaders of our century, said he felt that almost anything one can do will be insignificant. Yet to do *something* is very important. Each day, each chance is small but takes us in a direction. When we look back over the last month or last year, we may see that only remaining faithful to our program, one day at a time, has carried us a very long way. The kind of person we each become is just as important as what we accomplish in the world around us.

May I learn to have patience with the insignificant moments in the present. They are very important indeed.

I will thank you because I am marvelously made; your works are wonderful, and I know it well.

—Psalms 139:14

Some days we feel bad about ourselves. Perhaps there is no real reason except a mood has come over us. Moodiness is a remnant of our past. Or perhaps we feel guilty or ashamed or hurt. We feel blue. We feel grouchy toward ourselves or toward others around us and the world.

This is a time to turn it over to our Higher Power. We are children of the universe. We are loved. Our Creator has endowed us with marvelous strengths and potentials. Today may be a day we allow ourselves to be carried along by the love of our Higher Power. If we reach out we will feel the presence of the spirit in our contact with other people. We need not try so hard. We only need to pray for openness within ourselves to *feel* the love of God.

I pray for help today to renew the feeling within that God loves me and never abandons me.

Where there is no strife there is decay: "The mixture which is not shaken decomposes."
—*Heraclitus*

Transitions and changes are often painful, sometimes frightening. Often the most troubled lives are those most unyielding to change. When we become so committed to stability that we cannot flow with the never-ending river of life, we wither and die spiritually. Every one of us has changes moving within our lives. Some changes are beneath the surface and we only vaguely sense them. Others are obvious and we are dealing with their effects. When we see change only as a problem or as pain, we have a harder time getting on with our lives.

Looking back, we can see other changes we would never have chosen or planned for ourselves. We can see now that we grew with them. Change forced us into new realms, and we found sides of ourselves we hadn't known before. Through whatever strife and difficulty of change we face today, we have a stable program to fall back on. And we have our relationship with our Higher Power which is with us through all times.

I will try to have a lighter grip upon life today so that as the river of change flows, I can flow with it.

Words and magic were in the beginning one and the same thing, and even today words retain much of their magical power.
—Sigmund Freud

We shape our experiences with the words we use to describe them. Word images create expectations and we naturally move toward them. When a man says, "I can't!" he is commanding his unconscious self to be helpless. When he has a picture in his mind of moving toward his goal, he may say, "It's hard, but I'm going to give it my best effort." If, every time he makes a mistake, he mutters berating statements to himself like, "You idiot! You can't do anything right," he is teaching himself to be inadequate.

It's our responsibility in recovery to use respectful, honest, health-giving words. We can no longer use defeating, shaming, or derogatory words. Our language has a hypnotic effect on us and the people around us. So let's look at our resources today and name them. Let's meet our difficulties with our strength, our patience, and the backing of our Higher Power.

———

Today, I will call forth images and use words to show I respect myself and others.

A shortcut is often the quickest way to some place you weren't going.
—*Classic Crossword Puzzles*

We try shortcuts when we are in a hurry. The founders of this program tell us many people tried to find an easier, softer way because this one seemed too hard and too slow. Shortcuts to growth lead to dead ends and detours. Many men have experimented with shortcuts like "the geographical cure," "controlled use," "get-rid-of-this-partner-and-try-someone-else," "abstinence without the spiritual part of recovery," or "selecting some of the Steps and bypassing others."

The shortest road to one's own spirituality is the long road we see before us. We may wish for something more to our liking. But that is not an option for those of us who choose to grow toward full manhood. We deal with one day's—or one hour's—part of the road at a time. Maybe we see a job we have to do, a challenge to face, an unfinished talk with someone. Our task is to take this day and, in partnership with our Higher Power, see it in the light of our spiritual path.

I pray for faithfulness to this program. I will avoid shortcuts, allowing my spirituality to grow and deepen.

Come, Love! Sing On! Let me hear you sing this song—sing for joy and laugh, for I the creator am truly subject to all creatures.
—*Mechtild of Magdeburg*

Recovery without joy and song and playfulness is incomplete. The beauty of music uplifts our spirits and shows us the face of our Creator. For many men, music is their means of meditation and conscious contact with their Higher Power. When we experience the creativity of a musical piece, as it speaks to us, we take a step beyond the practical world, into the profound level of creation.

Some people say, "How can you celebrate when there is so much suffering, so much to grieve about?" We have grieved, we continue to grieve alongside our joy. But we need not pour all our energies into the painful and sad. Life is also wonderful. Music and dance and the joy of good fellowship enrich our lives and strengthen us to go on.

Praise the spirit of our Creator for all that is given to us!

I believe our concept of romantic love is irrational, impossible to fulfill, and the cause of many broken homes. No human being can maintain that rarified atmosphere of "true love."
—Rita Mae Brown

What the popular media teach us about marriage and love is poor preparation for the real thing. When we enter a relationship we may be filled with a feeling of magic and excitement of new love. But that is not a good basis for a lifelong commitment. Love at first sight is no reason for marriage. Many of us, upon meeting difficulties in our relationships, said to ourselves, "Maybe it wasn't true love after all, because now I don't feel in love with my mate anymore."

Honesty and learning how to resolve difficulties provide a solid foundation for durable love. Some relationships do not survive the honesty of recovery. Sometimes the development of honest love only begins with recovery. The love that endures, the love of real intimacy, comes when we know the real person. Loyalty to our loved ones may deepen as we deal more and more with reality.

As I grow in this program, married or single, I become more able to have an enduring love.

We learn more by seeing someone play good tennis than by reading a book about how to play good tennis.

—*W. Timothy Gallwey*

In our program we learn from each other. Most of us would rather have thought our problems through on our own or read about them without having to ask for help. Recovery requires us to break this old habit. We can no longer say at a meeting, "I had some problems this week, but I've worked them out now" or "I know what I have to do." The change for us is to ask for help from other men in this program. We need to say, "What do you think about my problem?" or "Would you be willing to talk to me for a while?"

Having a sponsor is an important way of getting to know how another man applies his program to his life. We need to select a sponsor we admire, who has learned the Steps well and who truly lives them. Then we need to spend time with our sponsor outside of meetings, perhaps while drinking a cup of coffee or going for a walk. By associating with others who are diligent about recovery, we will learn more than we could any other way.

Today, I will make personal contact with others in this program.

We are each so much more than what some reduce to measuring.
　　　　　　　　　　　—*Karen Kaiser Clark*

Our society places great emphasis on how well each person is doing. It makes us judgmental and competitive. As children we may have thought that our real value was measured by the grades we got in school or the scores of our baseball games. As grown men we continue measuring our worth by things like the size of our wages, the model of the car we drive, or even how many months or years we have in recovery.

We can't stop the measuring, but we are in a program that helps us step outside this system. We seek to know and do the will of our Higher Power, which is beyond the limitations of such measurements. Submitting our own will to our Higher Power releases us from the competition and the judgments in these games of measurement. Our loyalties are to values like honesty, respect, peace, and wholeness.

Today, I will remember that my value as a man isn't measured on a man-made scale.

Originality is unexplored territory. You get there by carrying a canoe—you can't take a taxi.
                                        —Alan Alda

We are on an adventure trip in this program. Each of us is a wilderness that is only partly explored and mapped. We can't know exactly what we will find along the way, but we can expect to find some great and moving beauty, some spectacular experiences, as well as awesome and frightening ones, and some soft, pleasant rest spots. Any day will have a mixture of various feelings.

This program is not a map of the uncharted territory. It is a guide for survival in the wilderness. It tells us how to orient ourselves when there are no familiar landmarks and how to learn and grow from the experience. The more time we spend in this wilderness, exploring the mystery of living, the more comfortable we become with it and the greater appreciation we have for its unique beauty.

Today, I pray for the courage to explore the original person I was created to be.

You must fight off a "bad luck" way of thinking as if you were dealing with an invasion of hostile forces—for that is precisely what you are dealing with.

—Maxwell Maltz

Life is an ongoing experience with two opposing forces. One force is constantly building up, and the other is constantly tearing down. We have successes and accomplishments, and we have failures and defeats. We finally get our house in order, and it immediately begins to become disordered again.

There are forces supporting our self-esteem and forces tearing us down. Friends who wish us well, goodwill and generosity among people, and the momentum of our healthy actions are constructive forces in our lives. Destructive forces are the pull of old habits, bad luck, accidents, and negative thoughts. We must choose on which side we will put our energies. Are we men who hate ourselves, believe in bad luck and despair, and thereby join the forces that would tear us down? Or will we choose to be on the side that builds us up?

Today, by the grace of God, I will join the forces that are on my side. I will stand up for myself and my worth.

The turning point in the process of growing up is when you discover the core of strength within you that survives all hurt.

—Max Lerner

When we consider all of the troubles and crises in our lives and all of the scrapes we've gotten into, we might feel overwhelmed. With what we have gone through, it seems miraculous for many of us to be here today. When we stop feeling sorry for ourselves and when we stop complaining about the unfairness of it all, we may get a new insight: "I have survived!"

We see the strength and persistence which brought us through the toughest times we have known. Even when some of us did not know it, we were being carried along by our Higher Power. We can draw strength from that knowledge. We can remind ourselves today that, knowing what we have lived through with the help of our Higher Power, we can deal with anything to come.

I am grateful to my Higher Power for help in surviving the hard times in life.

A father is a thousand schoolmasters.
                                    —Louis Nizer

We carry our fathers within us in ways we may not notice. When we do notice this in our thoughts and actions, we can use this relationship as a source of strength. When we hear a critical mental message saying we didn't perform well enough, is it a father's voice? When we feel a sense of strength and peace, are we in touch with our childhood knowledge of fatherly love? When we doubt our ability to get along with any woman, are we relying on what we learned in our childhood homes?

Perhaps we can recast our father-son relationship in adult terms. Were our fathers too removed from our lives for us to know them? Maybe we can see now that a father's love was there but was overshadowed by the demands of survival or by a misguided life. If we are forever seeking our fathers' approval, we may need to find the ways in which they are truly human and imperfect like us. Making peace with them—whether face-to-face or in the memory of a relationship—empowers us with their strengths and grants us the adulthood we deserve.

I will make peace with my father in my mind, and his strength and that of his father will be a well-spring in my life.

*It's not hard. When I'm not hittin', I don't hit
nobody. But when I'm hittin', I hit anybody!*
—Willie Mays

It seems like some days everything goes our way.
Everything falls together in a way that makes life easier for us. Other days are just the opposite; on a bad
day we seem to be all thumbs. In our spiritual practice
we know we don't control all that goes on around us.

We all are vulnerable to accidents, random misfor-
tune, and illness. Yet, when we don't fight against the
events of our lives, somehow things go better for us.
We can remember that as difficult as a day may be, we
are never alone because nothing can separate us from
our Higher Power. When we accept the bad things
that come, even though they are unfair, we give them
less power in our lives. Then we are free to go forward
and leave more room for the good things.

---

*Today, I'll accept the problems I must confront and leave
room for the good things.*

The loneliness each man feels is his hunger for life itself.... It is the yearning that makes fulfillment possible.

—Ross Mooney

Many different journeys have been taken by the men who finally entered this program in search of hope. Most of us have known our own brand of desperation, but we have one thing in common—the loneliness we felt. Some of us felt left out of our families and other groups. We were appalled by what was happening in our lives, alone with our secrets, as if no one truly knew us. Some of us even romanticized our loneliness as a form of heroism.

As we gave up our controlling behaviors, false pride, overcompetitiveness, and striving for power, we made our weak spots and secrets more obvious. We became more accessible to friends. As we count the blessings of recovery, high on our list is that we are no longer lonely.

In part, what kept me going and led me to this program was my hunger for life. I'm grateful for the friends who truly know me now, and still accept me.

Choice of attention—to pay attention to this and ignore that—is to the inner life what choice of action is to the outer. In both cases, a man is responsible for his choice and must accept the consequences.

—W. H. Auden

Many of us have said, "I can't help myself!" when we tried to stop our constant thinking about other people or their behavior. "I know it's not good for me, but what can I do when they keep acting that way?"

Let us think of ourselves as living in a house with many windows. At each window is a different view, and within each view are many things to catch our attention. Perhaps there are some people, some traffic, some buildings, a horizon, some trees. If we always go to the same window and focus on the same object, we are not using all our choices. We may have overlooked some things in our lives that need attention. There are many things we are totally powerless over. Our power exists in changing the focus of our attention.

Today, I will notice where I am choosing to pay attention. I pray for guidance in being aware of my options.

Although the world is full of suffering, it is also
full of the overcoming of it.

—*Helen Keller*

When a man looks at his life and at the lives of others, it is clear that pain is part of life. We cannot escape this tragic truth; our growth and our wholeness must include it because our recovery stresses honesty. In our old way of living, we may have been bitter. Many of us felt sorry for ourselves. Some of us cursed God and wasted time in our self-centeredness, thinking life was especially unfair to us. Life is not fair; it just is. It is left to us to choose how we will respond.

People's responses to life inspire us. We not only acknowledge the pain, but we see the heroic lives of others around us. They met their limitations and went forward with a willing spirit and faith. Today we can be grateful for the progress we have made in overcoming our suffering. We have friends who give us the joy of human contact. We have choices and possibilities where we never saw them before. We have a growing self-respect as men.

I accept the reality of life, and I will respond with faith in
the choices I make today.

"Wait'll next year!" is the favorite cry of baseball fans, football fans, hockey fans, and gardeners.
—*Robert Orben*

Hope was a casualty for many of us in our life of chaos and extremes. Some of us said to ourselves, "Life is just drab, I'd better get used to it." We may have slowly changed our definition of *normal* to mean a hopeless existence. Others of us held onto some shred of hope that said "Better times are just around the corner," but it only kept us from confronting how disastrous our lives had become. We are brothers in that we truly have been men on a dead-end path.

Our new lives have seen the dawning of true hope that has a solid base upon reality. We have the reality of friendships with our brothers and sisters. They provide comfort and support which are reliable and durable. We have the reality of our clearer thinking and our amended lives. We may not have everything we could desire, but we are actually on the road and progressing in directions we wish to go. We are engaged in the adventure of increasing our conscious contact with God. Our hope is founded in what we already feel in our lives.

Today, nothing is perfect, but hope underlies everything. With the return of hope, I have my life back again.

In the life of the Indian there is only one inevitable duty—the duty of prayer—the daily recognition of the Unseen and Eternal. He sees no need for setting apart one day in seven as a holy day, since to him all days are God's.
    —Ohiyesa, Santee Dakota

Some of our past troubles came from our naive arrogance. We failed to acknowledge anything beyond ourselves. Whatever was unseen or eternal remained invisible to us. We were skeptical, scientific, task-oriented, self-centered, unreflective. It's like we had been racing down a country highway at top speed, hardly tuned in to the rich vitality of life that surrounded us. When we stopped the car and explored the road banks, we could suddenly smell the grasses, hear birds singing, perhaps see a whole community in an anthill, or watch a darting squirrel.

Coming to believe in a Power greater than ourselves is not something we create on our own. It is largely a matter of shifting our attention, of being open to the spiritual. We don't need to force it. We need only be willing to quiet ourselves and notice. Ultimately, every moment is sacred.

Today, may I live from moment to moment.

My father didn't tell me how to live; he lived,
and let me watch him do it.
                              —Clarence Budinton Kelland

We learn much of what we need to know about being men from models we have in other men. Some of us have fond memories of being next to our fathers and imitating their ways. Many of us also have the feeling of a gap in our models. Perhaps our fathers weren't around enough, or we may have rejected some of their habits and values, creating an uncertainty about masculine roles. We may feel unsure of ourselves, or we may berate ourselves for what we don't know.

It is well to remember how much we have already learned in our adult years. It is never too late. No man ever reaches adulthood having learned everything from his father that he will need to know about masculinity. We can look around us for more models in the men we know. For a man to be our model, we first choose someone we admire and then get to know him well. In this way, we carry on the human tradition of one man learning from another.

I am continuing to grow, and I can learn from the men I know now.

He who conceals his disease cannot expect to be cured.

—Ethiopian proverb

Concealment and secrecy have been second nature to some of us. We may have felt that our masculinity kept us loners. Perhaps we said we were covering the truth for someone else's good. Maybe we could not bear to expose the truth because we feared the consequences. For some of us a lie came more automatically than the truth. Now we are learning to be open with our friends, and we are finding the healing effect of fresh air for our secrets.

Although it's frightening to stop tampering with the truth, it's also exciting to feel the power of honesty and to deal with the consequences of uncovering it. Perhaps we still have some secrets that erode our well-being. If so, we need to bring them into the open so we can live completely honest lives. When we let others know us as we really are, we are casting our lot with good health and recovery.

Today, I will make progress in my recovery by letting myself be fully known.

The only intrinsic evil is lack of love.
—*John Robinson*

When we have feelings of guilt or self-hate, we have spiritual problems. It is a time to turn to our program for help. In the early stages of recovery we may, at times, feel more shameful than we ever did before, simply because we are becoming honest about how we feel. We may even become ashamed of our guilty feelings, and then the problem escalates.

Lack of love for ourselves is at the heart of our problem. We cannot become self-loving by force of will, but we can stop being so willful by simply yielding to the care of a loving God. At those moments we do not feel deserving of love, but we can stop fending it off. Perhaps God's love is coming to us in the concern of a friend or partner. Maybe it comes in the warm sunshine or in the smile of a child. As we yield to it, we take a spiritual leap into a world we don't control and we didn't create, but we can be healed by it.

Today, I will surrender to the love which comes from the world around me and let it teach me how to love myself.

Some people greet the morning with a smile, but it's more natural to protest its presence with sleepy sulkiness. "Who asked you to come again?" we feel like saying to it, as if it were a most unwelcome guest.

—*Brendan Francis*

We begin with the truth and build on the firm foundation it provides. We often hear we *should* have a positive attitude, we should be grateful for the new day. Perhaps some days we feel enthusiasm, and it's wonderful when we do. But we don't need to turn it into a requirement because shoulds tend to keep us out of touch with our honest feelings.

All feelings are acceptable. Whatever they are, the entire range of color and intensity of feelings comes from our Creator. Our task is dealing with them and responding to them. We begin by acknowledging them as they are. We do not have license to do whatever we feel like doing, only to feel what we feel. This point of honesty is a solid stepping-stone to grow from. We often find we feel different as soon as we admit our feelings.

Today, I will admit my true feelings and accept them as stepping-stones.

God is near me (or rather in me), and yet I may be far from God because I may be far from my own true self.

—C. E. Rolt

Our relationship with God and our relationship with ourselves are always interwoven. Sometimes we feel disconnected from ourselves or emotionally flat. We may block the flow of communication with our deeper selves by trying to evade a difficult or painful truth. At those times we grope for some kind of contact and may even ask, "Where is God?"

God is always with us, but sometimes we are the missing party. In the past, most of us were deeply alienated from ourselves and from our Higher Power. Our first moments of spiritual awakening may have been when we saw how far we were from our true selves. This honest message from ourselves to ourselves was painful but was also a recontact with the truth that made it possible to find God.

I need not ask where God is because God is loving and always near. I only need to ask, "Where am I?"

The tremor of awe is the best in man.

—Goethe

We have a spiritual experience in knowing and being touched by something much larger than us, something beyond what we understand, something of mysterious dimensions. It can happen as we stand on the banks of an ageless river, listen to beautiful music, read scripture, or say a prayer with a friend. When we set aside defiance, willfulness, and our demands to subdue whatever we meet, we become receptive to a larger reality. The experience of awe brings out the best in a man because it instills a spirit of respect and gratitude. It inspires humility and expands our minds into realms we can't express in words.

The sense of awe is a kind of reverence. After we learn where our personal awe is inspired, we can return to it again and again. As we feel it more, we become more open to it in the mundane parts of our daily lives. Today we might feel the spirit in the visit of a wild bird on a branch, the spontaneous "Hi" from a small child, or the stillness before prayer at the dinner table.

Today, I will look for moments of awe in my life.

We fear our highest possibility (as well as our lowest one). We are generally afraid to become that which we can glimpse in our most perfect moments.

—*Abraham Maslow*

In our daily lives, we may dream of success and achievement. We strive and compete in the workplace. We go to meetings and do our part on each Step in the program searching for better lives. When success comes, we are faced with a new problem we could not have expected. It comes as an outcome of some hard work, some good luck, and some help from our friends. It is frightening to have a good thing in our lives and not be in control of it.

We are just as powerless over our successes as we are over the worst of our behaviors. We can only be faithful to ourselves and our duties. The successes which flow from our work come and go. Since we can't nail them down, they may make us feel insecure. Many a man has destroyed his moment of success because he couldn't stand the powerless feeling. We must return to our program and allow success to rise and fall as it will.

Today, I turn to my Higher Power for help in accepting success.

A good indignation brings out all one's powers.
—Ralph Waldo Emerson

Anger is a human emotion that gets us in touch with our energy and our vitality. But like any good thing, it can also be used in hurtful ways. When we examine the role anger has played in our lives, some of us can see where we used it to intimidate and dominate others. Maybe we can recall being terrified by someone else's anger or even by our own. Some of us denied our anger and covered it with excessive helpfulness.

Examining the place anger has had in our lives is one of the doorways we must pass through to regain our full masculine spirit. We learn to set aside the anger we used to cover fear or hurt. We express it respectfully and honestly when we feel it in a relationship. Expressing anger does not have to be abusive or rejecting. It can mean we care enough to be fully involved and we will not leave after we express it. We can learn to hear others in their anger rather than attempt to control or evade their message. In the process we are invigorated and feel healthier because we are claiming a larger part of ourselves.

Today, I will first be honest with myself about angry feelings. Then I will find respectful ways to express them.

There is nothing as easy as denouncing. It don't take much to see that something is wrong, but it takes some eyesight to see what will put it right again.

—*Will Rogers*

We come to this day with a choice of whether to be for something or against it. Shall we put energy into what we seek and admire or shall we give our energy to opposition and resistance of what we dislike? If someone asks a favor, we have a choice to resent and resist the intrusion or to engage with the person and see where it might lead. If a project we are working on is frustrating, we can wallow in criticizing it or try to get a clearer picture of what will work and what we want.

Criticizing may be a helpful first stage in learning, but it is seductive because it holds little risk and we feel safe doing it. In that comfort we forget to go forward to create what we really want. Our negative energy, when we are seduced by it, creates negative results. When we look back upon today, we will admire those choices that risked creating something positive.

Today, I will not give my energy to denouncing but to creating what I believe is worthwhile.

JULY

If you are seeking creative ideas, go out walking. Angels whisper to a man when he goes for a walk.

—Raymond Inmon

We all seek creative ideas from time to time—perhaps when we have a problem resting heavily on our minds, or when we are simply in a bad mood. We need to refresh ourselves at those times. Refreshment doesn't solve a problem, but it can revitalize our thinking. Sometimes when we are feeling hopeless, we neglect to care for ourselves, forgetting a better environment will give us a stronger attitude, even toward the most difficult problems.

We must learn our own best methods for being refreshed—ways that allow angels to whisper to us. They should be simple, inexpensive, and accessible daily. Going for a walk is a very good example. Daily reading and study is another possibility. Observing nature, doing handicrafts or hobbies are refreshing for some men. These activities allow us to temporarily set aside our tasks and concerns and open us to creative ideas.

Today, I will give myself a creative break from the concerns I am facing.

Fair play is primarily not blaming others for anything that is wrong with us.
—*Eric Hoffer*

As adults, we accept responsibility for our feelings and our circumstances. We haven't chosen our own troubles, but we have the job of dealing with them. If a man falls and breaks a leg, he might say to someone, "It's your fault, and I'll make you pay for this!" But that won't fix his leg. The healing still has to come from within.

Our impulse to blame others is an attempt to escape our responsibilities. We become overcritical. We want someone else to take the rap for our pain and our misdeeds, but this only delays our wholeness as men. There is no point in blaming ourselves either. When we first confront our discomfort directly and accept responsibility for dealing with it, we feel an inner urge to escape again. If we stay with the discomfort a while, a new stage begins—the healing and acceptance stage. A feeling of wholeness comes, a feeling of being a real person, of having reached our full size.

May I not indulge in blame today—toward myself or anyone else. Instead, may I be a strong, responsible man.

Vitality shows not only in the ability to persist but in the ability to start over.
— F. Scott Fitzgerald

Sitting in a stalled car on the railroad tracks with a train approaching, one needs to let go and start over. A man who persists in that situation will die. Many situations require fierce persistence, but in others we need to start over. Early in recovery, most of us haven't had a good way of knowing the difference. Perhaps with every challenge we tried harder and held on tighter. Our codependent relationships and our addictions had been our escapes.

Often we long for some clear directions from God to tell us, "Now is the time to let go," or "Now is the time to persist." That is not how we hear from our Higher Power. We can practice being less automatic in rising to every challenge. We can learn to see the wisdom and vitality in starting over. Certainly our recovery is a good example. Gradually we develop our contact with our Higher Power to help discern the difference. As we do, we develop more options for leading healthier lives.

Today, I will not automatically persist with a challenge. I will notice when I have an opportunity to let go.

Freedom means the right to be different, the right to be oneself.

—Ira Eisenstein

Each of us is a unique creature and has special gifts to contribute to the world. We were not free in the past because we were slaves to addictions and codependency. We know that freedom is precious. Compulsions and pressures for conformity stifle our creativity and erode our dignity. As we grow in our relationship to our Higher Power, we get stronger and more balanced in our unique qualities. Some of us have a talent for empathizing with others, some for writing and art, others for sports and physical activities.

There is no recipe that prescribes exactly what kind of men we should be. Because we're free, it is our creative task to discover what it means to be honest, masculine, contributing men within our particular circumstances. We don't get a list of directions for each day, only guidelines for progress. Through groups and friendships, we develop in our own ways and learn to respect each other's freedom.

I am grateful for the freedom to be uniquely and fully myself.

We shall describe conditions of the soul that words can only hint at. We shall have to use logic to try to corner perspectives that laugh at our attempt.

—*Huston Smith*

As we live the spiritual life, we find words and logic are only capable of pointing in the direction of some truths. Words do not contain the entire truth our experience may be teaching us. This is like the difference between hearing about fishing versus actually being on the water, smelling the misty air, and feeling the fish tug on our line.

Spiritual development is a form of education. We are developing the part of us that learns by experience, that has a feeling without exactly knowing why, that understands stories better than statistics. Gradually, we accept more experiences in our lives as mysteries, as not fitting into any specific categories. Many experiences will have more meaning than cold facts could ever express. As this side of us develops, we don't discard reason and judgment; we become deeper human beings.

Today, I will give my intuition more freedom. That will help my spiritual self grow.

Is the inventor of the ear unable to hear? Is the creator of the eye unable to see?
— *Psalms 94:9*

The way we have been restored to our spiritual path is partly a mystery. Our willingness to accept mystery in our lives has taught us we are part of a larger whole. There is more at work in the world than we can know. Acceptance of the larger whole restores us to health.

We are not just separate beings with a private world. Our existence is part of a larger process. We came into being with no control and no forethought on our own part. We arise from a past that no one remembers.

It was when we didn't see our place—as part of creation—that we were in the greatest pain and difficulty. Now each day, each hour, when we remember we are not in charge, and our will is not in control, we are restored again.

I am thankful for the mystery of recovery. I accept this mystery as part of all the mysteries beyond my control.

Those who are mentally and emotionally healthy
are those who have learned when to say yes,
when to say no, and when to say whoopee!
—Willard S. Krabill

We men have fallen into many difficulties because of poorly defined personal boundaries. Some of us never learned to say no to our mothers and felt invaded or ruled by them. Or we never truly said no to our fathers—never went through a teenage rebellion to establish ourselves as adults. Others have gotten stuck saying no and have never learned to yield and say yes.

Boundary problems have been part of the difficulty in many areas of our lives. We've told ourselves we have no right to our yes or no, or we've said we're strong enough to sacrifice for someone else, or we've welcomed the escape from ourselves in discarding our choice. Not saying no when we needed to or not saying yes when we wanted to has led many of us into doctors' offices, courts, jails, lost jobs, divorces, and bad marriages. Now the inner voice of our Higher Power is showing us our limits and encouraging us to stand up for them.

I am learning to know myself by defining my boundaries and choosing when and when not to cross them.

*He was shut out from all family affairs. No one
told him anything. The children, alone with their
mother, told her all about the day's happenings,
everything. . . . But as soon as the father came
in, everything stopped.*

—D. H. Lawrence

Many of us men are on the outer edge of our family
circles. The closeness between our children and our
wives often seems more comfortable, more intimate
than our relationships with them. Perhaps it's similar
to the closeness we had with our mother while our
father was outside. It is painful to us and probably
not entirely our own fault. We were taught that our
main job was outside the home—supporting our family by earning a living. But it is up to us to change the
situation.

Many of us learned from our own father that grown
men stay aloof from emotional relationships, but this
has hurt our relationships and alienated us from the
people we most care for. Learning to know our feelings and how to express them helps us move into the
family circle of intimacy.

*Today, I will let go of my aloofness with my family so they
can know me better.*

The ultimate result of shielding men from the effects of folly is to fill the world with fools.
—Herbert Spencer

We sometimes wish we could protect friends or loved ones from the consequences of their actions. We'd like to pick up the pieces after they've made a mess of their lives. Or we fail to look at the dark side of someone's motives because we want only the best. Perhaps it is our controlling willfulness that tries to make things into what we want, rather than accepts things as they really are.

In our masculine recovery, a deeper love allows us to have a respectful distance from others. When we truly care about someone, we don't snatch them out of their learning experience. When we allow our loved ones and friends to confront the natural consequences of their own actions, they learn and grow just as we do. We can be with a friend, but we are no one's Higher Power.

Today, I will be respectful of others by letting them walk their path while I walk mine.

Fears are educated into us, and can, if we wish, be educated out.

                —Karl A. Menninger

Two of the problems common to men in this program are fear and lack of trust. Many of us have unconsciously enlarged our fears and returned to them again and again. Do we dwell excessively on fears? Are we too fearful about our health? Money? Jobs? Love? Jealousy? The future? What other people think?

Many of us are victims of our fears and anxieties. Fears in moderation are healthy signals to us. But we need to learn to be more trusting. We can simply open ourselves to the possibility that things will turn out well. We don't need to be blind to the negatives—only have our eyes less fixed on them. No one can ever prove to us that it is finally safe to trust.

Fearfulness is the problem, not any one fear. Trusting our Higher Power, we set our fearfulness aside, even if a few particular fears remain.

Today, I will be open to learn about trust.

In playing, and perhaps only in playing, the child or adult is free to be creative.
—*D. W. Winnicott*

There are so many activities called play which have not really been playful. Organized sports for youth which consumed some of us are called play. The partying which was connected with some of our addictions is called play. Reckless and dangerous driving is called play. In recovery, some of us become intensely focused on doing what's right, and we need a deeper understanding to take the spiritual leap into creative play.

This leap takes a willingness to let go. Maybe we remember hurtful things happening when our guard was down. Creative play involves trusting that every activity doesn't need a worthy goal, doesn't need to be planned out. Pleasure, humor, lightness, and aimless passing of time are forms of openness to the spirit of God. It is experimenting, exploring, setting aside our ordered and planned approach to most of life, and accepting that what comes out will be all right.

God, help me see the possibilities for play in the moments of this day.

If you keep on saying things are going to be bad,
you have a good chance of being a prophet.
                              —Isaac Bashevis Singer

Many of us have the habit of taking a negative out-look on whatever comes along. We don't believe things will work out for us; we don't think we will have a good day; we can't accept our friends' warm feelings. To follow this gloomy path is a strange dis-tortion of faith—it is faith in the negative. Any fore-cast, whether hopeful or pessimistic, is a step into the unknown. So why do we choose the dark one?

We get a payoff for our pessimism which keeps us hooked. It creates misery, but serves our demand for control. There is more risk in being open to something positive because we cannot force positive things to oc-cur. We can only be open to them and believe in the possibility. But when we predict the negative and ex-pect only bad things, we squelch many good things or overlook them. Then we say, "I knew it would be this way," and in our misery we satisfy our self-centered craving to be in charge. When we surrender our need to be in control, we are more open and welcoming of the good things that come our way.

Today, I will be open to the good that is around me.

If I were to begin life again, I should want it as it was. I would only open my eyes a little more.
—Jules Renard

Spiritual and emotional growth is a process of raising our awareness. Reflecting on our growth as men, before this program and after, we see different levels of consciousness. Some of us might say we weren't at all conscious of what it meant to be a man by the time we entered the adult world.

Now we are forming an awareness of manhood. We see ourselves more as recovering, caring, strong, vulnerable men in relationships with others. We have an increased sense that our actions make a difference as sons, as fathers, as husbands, lovers, and friends. Our increased understanding of ourselves makes it possible to fulfill our potentials for growth. It is not idle fantasy to imagine beginning life again because, in a sense, we have. In recovery, it seems we have begun life again, only with our eyes a little more open.

Help me live this day with all of my awareness.

*Life is not a "brief candle." It is a splendid torch
that I want to make burn as brightly as possible
before handing on to future generations.*
—*George Bernard Shaw*

We are men who have sought intensity. Some have
said the extremes of our past were a kind of search for
a Higher Power, although we went to self-defeating
ends. There is no need now for us to give up our intense love of life. Serenity need not be bland. In facing
ourselves, confronting our pain, surrendering our arrogant individualism, we are released to live the life
we deeply desire.

What do men really want? We want to have true,
lasting friendships with other men and women—to be
at peace with ourselves and our Higher Power. We
want to be fully aware in the present moments of our
lives. We want to have some joy and to make a contribution to the world.

---

*I am grateful that my torch burns brightly. I am finding
what I really want.*

There is nothing you can say in answer to a compliment. I have been complimented myself a great many times, and they always embarrass me—I always feel that they have not said enough.

—Mark Twain

Hearing the good words and praise of another person is harder for some of us to accept than criticism and abuse. Perhaps it is easier to receive what we are accustomed to, or maybe we feel a loss of control when someone compliments us. This is a time for us to begin accepting others' actions. We do not need to be in control of our relationships at all times. When friends offer sincere compliments, we don't need to push them away or brush them off.

All we need to do is allow others' positive messages to come into us. In a good relationship we listen to the feelings of our friends, and sometimes that means truly listening as they tell us their good feelings about us.

Today, I will be open to the compliments that come my way without controlling them.

Do not seek death. Death will find you.
—Dag Hammarskjöld

When we accept deep within ourselves the fact that we will die, that our days are numbered as certainly as those of each thriving, bustling generation before us, then we become more fully alive and vital men. Facing this raises grief over our loss, and we wish to avoid it. Yet, death keeps us honest. It highlights the folly of our questions about whether we should live or die and confronts us with the self-destructive behaviors we have used. Some of us have nearly killed ourselves by our extreme behaviors.

Since death is certain, the real question is, *How shall we live?* By pursuing recovery and spiritual growth we have chosen to live more fully and to use our energies well. We live with commitment to our highest values. We stay in tune with our inner voice to help us make choices. We play, we love, and we celebrate the miracle of life every day, not because there is no grief, but because life is precious and time is limited.

Today, I will accept my grief over the limits of life. I will celebrate its wonder.

*I loafe and invite my soul, I lean and loafe at my
ease observing a spear of summer grass.*
—*Walt Whitman*

How foreign the thought is to many men that we
might make progress by loafing. Yet we probably have
experienced it. We have felt more in tune with ourselves after taking a break. After an especially relaxing
weekend we feel more alive or more clear about ourselves. At those times we have invited our soul and
have been rejuvenated.

Centuries of spiritual practice from different ideol-
ogies have taught the need for quiet relaxation in
some form to invite the soul. Some have practiced a
Sabbath day each week, others a time of prayer every
day—even several times a day—others have practiced
a daily period of deep meditation. Simply a period of
loafing, with no particular goal in mind, may invite
conscious contact with our Higher Power.

---

*I pray for the ability to set aside my busy pace of life, my
worrying and fretting, my "take charge" attitude for a
period of time today.*

How should one live? Live welcoming to all.
—Mechtild of Magdeburg

Welcoming is a spiritual practice we met when we came to this program. We may recall our first meetings and how welcome we felt in this group of fellow sufferers. It gave us hope when we felt desperate and continues to provide us with a nourishing place to grow.

To be welcoming means to accept others as they are, without passing judgment on their worth. It means to encourage them when they are despairing and to accept that they have a rightful place in our world. Welcoming is being generous with our resources. We do not have to feel close to someone to be welcoming. We can welcome a stranger. As we practice this attitude toward others, regardless of their status in life, regardless of their good or bad actions, we are changed inside. We learn from the people we welcome, and we are reminded that in the sight of God we are all loved as equals.

Today, I will practice a welcoming attitude toward everyone I meet.

They have rights who dare defend them.
—Roger Baldwin

There is a hard side to emotional health and manhood. As we grow, we gain many more sides, more ways of responding to the situations we meet. We learn that yielding to God sometimes means letting our full strength flow to defend our rights and ward off intrusion or disrespect. As we have become more loving and tolerant, we have become more assertive for our rights and those of others.

We must speak up for ourselves and for our points of view. We must not let others demean us or put us down, nor can we take on blame for others' life problems. When we ought to stand up for ourselves and don't, we may be invaded by a false feeling that we are crazy or bad. As recovering men, we sometimes must call on our hard side and say, "No! I will not be a doormat for the harmful actions of others. I will defend my rights."

I will cultivate my relationship with my Higher Power and let that lead me to stand up for myself.

Without solitude there can be no real people. . . . The measure of your solitude is the measure of your capacity for communion.
—John Eudes

If we listen in those moments when we hear a message from ourselves, we become true men—real human beings. The message comes in our solitude, when our defenses against truth are set aside. It comes popping out without our planning it. Our solitude is a relationship with ourselves, and it might occur in silent meditation, or driving down the street, or during a dinner conversation. The message might be a painful truth like, "You just acted like a small child," or a frightening fact like, "You are deeply loved by another person."

Letting another person know what messages we are getting in solitude helps us deal with the messages. As we accept our imperfections and make peace with ourselves, we increase our sense of solitude. We become real men, full partners in relationships and in our communities.

Today, I will welcome solitude. When the messages from myself are painful or frightening, I will be gentle with myself.

Some people regard themselves as perfect, but only because they demand little of themselves.
—Hermann Hesse

Many of us men in this program have a struggle with perfectionism. This is a central spiritual issue. Sometimes we feel ashamed or frightened by our imperfections, or we strive so hard to overcome them that we successfully close our lives down to a very narrow, controllable scale. Spiritual awakening means we have zest for life and accept our imperfections.

We know today will be shaky and insecure in some ways. We probably will make some mistakes or offenses. Our solution is not our old behavior of attempting to control whatever happens; it is to join life with a spiritual feeling. We let go of ourselves, and what happens? We are part of a larger whole. We are not in control of the process of life, and whatever we do is part of an ongoing dialogue, so we will have another chance to respond, even to our own mistakes.

Today, I pray for liberation from my perfectionism so I can more fully engage in life's adventure.

Suffering is a journey which has an end.
—Matthew Fox

Pain is part of life. To live a masculine spiritual life, we need a way to understand the suffering we sometimes endure. Looking back at other difficult times can give us a better perspective of the pain we feel today. All of us can recall a loss or a sudden difficult change that we never would have chosen for ourselves. Perhaps it brought us face-to-face with insecurities or doubts about our survival. Now, after the suffering has ended, we see how much we grew. We changed; we were strengthened and, perhaps, were liberated by what happened to us.

Thoughts about today's suffering may not be clear as to what good it holds for us. But we are on a journey, and it can only happen one step at a time. We know that journeys teach us great lessons and they do have endings. Our pain today affirms that we are vital and alive people. We know others suffer as we do, and we can turn to each other to give and receive comfort while we are on the journey.

My pain will teach me something I need to know, and it will have an end. I will pay attention to its lessons.

He that to what he sees, adds observation, and to what he reads, reflection, is in the right road to knowledge.

—*Caleb Colton*

We are not just feathers blown on the winds of a powerless life. We bring ourselves to our experiences. The dynamics of learning include, first, what happens —what we see or read or hear—and, second, what we make of it. So in our observations and reflections we consider what an event means to us.

As men in a spiritual program, we need some time to think and reflect. That is, we need time away from the phone, away from interruptions and work, where we can let ourselves learn and grow from our experiences. Some men get that by leaving the radio off while driving alone, others get it on the bus, others light a candle in a quiet room at home and meditate. In this way we are conscious and aware of what is happening in our lives and we bring our wisdom to it. Through time we deepen and grow stronger as we grow older rather than only accumulating more experiences.

Today, I will reflect on the meaning of my experiences and bring my wisdom to them.

Many things are lost for want of asking.
—English proverb

It's a principle of this program that we grow, in part, by learning to ask for what we need. Perhaps today we are struggling with a problem that could be eased if we talked to another man in the program. We could call him on the phone and just ask him if he has a few minutes to talk. Maybe we're wondering about a physical pain. Maybe we feel strange about something we said and would like to ask someone's opinion.

Mistaken notions about masculinity get in the way of recovery when we refuse to ask for help. We think we should know the answers and be self-sufficient. Maybe we feel stupid if we have to ask. Those notions drop by the wayside as we get healthier and learn the rewards of connecting with others to satisfy our mutual needs. No longer does false pride have to keep us isolated and struggling alone.

Today, I will notice what I need and practice asking for help.

Everyone once, once only. Just once and no more. And we also once. Never again. But this having been once, although only once, to have been of the earth, seems irrevocable.
—*Rainer Maria Rilke*

In the hopelessness of addiction and codependency, and as children of addicts, some of us have considered suicide, and some of us have actually tried to kill ourselves. We have maintained the option as an escape in case life got too difficult. Now, in recovery, we have chosen life. We've stopped killing ourselves in the slow ways of our old behaviors, yet some of us hold on to our ace in the hole. Either consciously or unconsciously, we haven't made that unconditional commitment to life.

It may be one more firm step into recovery—a vote for the life we have been given—to say, "I will never choose suicide. Whatever comes my way, it is not an option for me." When we give up that one final controlling maneuver, we may find ourselves freer to live in this one irretrievable life we've been given.

In choosing to be totally on the side of life, I step further into the care of God. Whatever I must meet, God is with me.

The lust for power is not rooted in strength but in weakness.

—*Erich Fromm*

Many of us have felt so insecure, so poor, or so much the underdog that we made a fervent promise to ourselves that we'd come out on top later. We know how weak we felt, and that image continues to be our guiding force long after the weakness was overcome. We may have spiritual problems because we are blind to the reality of our present life. While grasping for more security, more love, more money, or trying to lose more weight or attract more friends, we fail to stop and realize the real rewards we already have today. We are driven by the memory of pain and insecurity, rather than rising above it and relating to the higher principles and people around us. Our spiritual problems are not solved by getting more control or more achievements, but by making peace with the fact that life is insecure.

Today, I will let go of my grasping for more. I will let go of it again and again throughout the day so I am not ruled by this weakness.

You cannot get it by taking thought;
You cannot seek it by not taking thought.
                                    —Zenrin poem

We are transported into unfamiliar worlds in this program by ideas that sometimes confound our mind. In the spiritual realms we learn things we didn't learn anywhere else, and gradually they bring us peace. We can decide with our will to follow a spiritual direction, to turn our life and will over to the care of our God. We cannot control what God will do with them. When we learn that part of our problem was trying too hard, being too self-sufficient, or being too controlling, our old ways tell us to try hard to control that. But then we are only doing more of the same old thing. We learn that after making our decision, our Higher Power takes over. Now it is possible to be released from our own trying, to move beyond our own efforts by falling into the caring hand of God.

I must give this program first priority in my life, remembering my spiritual progress comes as a gift, not as an achievement.

I am ill because my mind is in a rut and refuses to leave.

—*Karen Giordino*

We are vulnerable human beings. We are susceptible to accidents and disease, and we can get bogged down in unhealthy thinking. We aren't at fault when we catch a cold or get a more serious illness, and accidents can happen to anyone. In the same way our addictions and the addictions of people we are close to are not our fault. We never asked for these afflictions, yet we must deal with them.

Physical and spiritual health can't be separated. A thriving spiritual life creates an environment for physical healing and strength. In the same way, physical well-being infuses our spirit with hope and joy. Human beings cannot go through life without sometimes being ill in either mind or body. Living by this program helps make us healthier in all ways. When we are bogged down, we can turn to one of the Steps as a means of healing and release.

Today, I will remember that I am a whole man, with body and spirit as one. As I turn to the Steps, my whole being is healed.

Change and growth take place when a person has risked himself and dares to become involved with experimenting with his own life.
—*Herbert Otto*

The rewards of our new life are apparent to us because of how we feel, and apparent to others by what they can see. Many of us had reached our bottom point, and we felt there was no risk in trying a program of recovery. Yet, we still had some distorted security in our harmful ways of relating to others or in our addictions. Letting go was an experiment. This program gives us guidelines for experimenting with our life for growth, and we continue growing every day.

Some of our benefits are increased confidence and self-respect, more intimacy with our partner, better friendships, and better physical health. We feel these changes in ourselves, and we see them in the other men and women in this program.

Today, I am grateful for the rewards in my life from this experiment in recovery.

Many could forego heavy meals, a full wardrobe, a fine house, et cetera; it is the ego they cannot forego.

—*Mohandas Gandhi*

We inevitably confront our ego in this program. We face our macho self, our powerful self, or our always-right self. We have developed many trappings which give us an identity: our car, our stereo system, our job, our popularity, or our place to sit in church. The more attached we are to these trappings, the tougher it is for us to make progress on this spiritual path.

In stepping across a stream we must leave the side we are on in order to get to the other side. The repeated challenge in our spiritual life is to leave the secure trappings we know and take comfort in the still unknown new self. That is the leap of faith. We take the risk and trust something will be there for us. We have faith that letting go of our immediate attachments will bring us to a better place, that God will be there for us.

I will let go of external images and use my faith to take the leap forward.

Look at the past as a bullet. Once it's fired it's finished.

—Catherine Bauby

Today is before us as an unformed experience. Yesterday took its own shape, and whatever it was has now gone. Our only opportunities exist in what we will do this day. Perhaps we can enhance the day by starting with a review of yesterday and then letting go. What were the major events in our experiences yesterday? How do we feel about them? Is something left unfinished in our feelings or actions that we need to complete or repair today? Can we take yesterday's experience to build a better today?

We have centered ourselves in this day by reviewing where we just came from. We have taken a spot check inventory. Now we can let go of yesterday and move forward in the present. That does not mean we never think about the past again. It means we build on the past by learning from our experiences and letting them shape our activities now. In that way we draw ever closer into accord with the will of our Higher Power.

I will let go of the past by learning from it. I give myself to shaping today.

AUGUST

The great artist is the simplifier.
                                    —*Henri Amiel*

Just as an artist creates through simplification, so a man's recovery process grows and deepens as he simplifies his life. This isn't easy to do in our fast-paced and high-powered world. We have often complicated a problem by our way of thinking. Sometimes we take pride in how complex we can make something seem. We look for hidden meanings when the truth is on the surface. We give long explanations for our actions when none is called for. We suspect a person's motives when nothing is lost by taking him at face value. We take on a battle when we could just as well let it pass.

Most of us don't think of ourselves as artists. Yet we are each given a profound, creative opportunity—to fashion a meaningful and worthwhile pattern in our lives. As we seek to do the will of God today, it is as if we are taking a lump of clay and creating an image from it.

As I go about today's activities, may I find ways to make it a simple and creative expression.

Every closed eye is not sleeping, and every open eye is not seeing.

—*Bill Cosby*

Things are not always as they seem, even with ourselves. Sometimes we get settled into a routine in our program. We are beyond the early struggles with detachment and sobriety. We have encountered many of the benefits of recovery. We attend our meetings and we know the words and ideas of the program. Although it all looks good on the outside, when we're honest with ourselves, we know our spirit has gone flat. This is a serious situation and needs our attention.

When the inside feeling does not match our outside appearance, we need to become vulnerable again. We need to talk about how we really feel. Maybe little secrets we have been holding have deadened our program. Perhaps we haven't admitted a pain in our life. Maybe we have been seduced by the power of looking good and have traded away the genuineness of being known by our friends. The renewal of this program is something we feel from within, and we can continue to be renewed.

I pray my eyes will be open to see and my program will stay alive and genuine.

To live a spiritual life we must first find the courage to enter into the desert of loneliness and to change it by gentle and persistent efforts into a garden of solitude.

—Henri J. M. Nouwen

Knowing our loneliness and admitting it to ourselves is the beginning of a spiritual path for many men. Today we are on a spiritual journey. We already have the means to translate the pain of our loneliness into a deeper spiritual dimension. Most men in this program came in deeply aware of their feelings of isolation. Now, with the companionship of our Higher Power, we can spend time alone and use it for spiritual growth. As we develop a relationship with ourselves and deepen our knowledge of our Higher Power, our loneliness transforms into solitude.

In this quiet moment today, we can be more accepting of ourselves than we were in the past. We admit loneliness has caused us pain, but now we can see that it also can lead us to our deeper self where we find serene solitude. This change is a movement into the spiritual world.

Thanks to God for the solitude I have found in my life.

The craftsman does not always build toward a prior vision. Often images come in the process of working. The material, his hands—together they beget.

—M. C. Richards

We awaken in the morning, and the day is an un-built creation. We have some ideas about what we will accomplish today. But our Higher Power also has some things in mind which are not yet part of our consciousness. We have lived long enough to know that every day brings surprises. We know in advance we will be frustrated in some of our desires, and we may be helped or advanced in others. But what about the totally unexpected? Will we even notice the subtle opportunities? Will we see an opportunity for a friendly conversation? Do our plans unwittingly prevent other possibilities from intruding?

When we hold loosely to our daily plans, we are more open to knowing the will of our Higher Power. Then each day is a spiritual process. It becomes a combined creation of our Higher Power and our own consciousness.

Today, I will hold my own plan loosely so that I can continue to be open to the healing powers of God.

The whole problem is to establish communication with one's self.

—E. B. White

We are like many-faceted gemstones. Each side represents a different aspect of ourselves. We have our emotional sides with different feelings and responses. We have our competencies and strengths, hopes and desires, destructiveness and negativity, self-doubts and resentments. We also possess a drive for power and knowledge, a desire to serve, and a wish to connect with others.

Our spiritual masculinity requires that we know our many sides. We need a working relationship with our thoughts and feelings so they can be appreciated, accepted, and understood. When we tell our story in a meeting, we let others know us, and we get to know ourselves better. When we are spontaneous in what we say or do, we communicate with ourselves. We discover ourselves through meditation, journal writing, playfulness, physical activity, and conversations with others. In that way we become more honest.

Today, I will use my lines of communication with myself and become more self-accepting and more honest.

*God respects me when I work, but he loves me
when I sing.*
—*Rabindranath Tagore*

We seek balance in our lives. The greatest sign of
unmanageability in our past was the unbalanced lives
we led. This is no easy lesson to learn. We are inclined
to grasp for a single answer, thinking we now have the
key insight to a happier way of life. As men, many of
us have pursued our happiness in work with little
time for anything else. Perhaps, for some, the singing
and playing we have done were part of our addiction
or participating with someone else in their addiction.
This makes it feel dangerous or frightening now to be
playful in recovery.

We can find ways to have more balance in our lives.
Spiritual vitality grows when we make room in our
day for lighthearted play as well as the serious tasks.

*I pray for guidance from my Higher Power to help me find
a balance in my life today.*

We love because it's the only true adventure.
—Nikki Giovanni

In loving, we meet ourselves. As we have become more honest, we no longer make excuses about our relationship problems. We can't blame our troubles on our partner. Our problems with love were often because we didn't know how to be close or we didn't dare to be.

When we let ourselves engage in this adventure, we meet many obstacles—things we can't control, and sometimes we want to quit right there. We have arguments and disappointments as well as good feelings. But what adventure is without difficulty or surprises? Part of the reason for choosing new experiences is to confront forces outside our control. A relationship is a dialogue. Only if we stay with it through the frustrations, express our deepest feelings openly, and listen to our partner, do we achieve a new level of understanding and confidence in the relationship. Then deeper levels also open within ourselves.

Today, I will let honesty guide me in this adventure of my love dialogue.

I got the blues thinking of the future, so I left off and made some marmalade. It's amazing how it cheers one up to shred oranges and scrub the floor.

—D. H. Lawrence

Focusing on pain or having difficulties can put us in a rut, and we neglect the other things in our lives. A simple task like making marmalade can be a brief vacation. We change our thought patterns when we change activities. The simple action of doing something pleasant might inject a new feeling into our outlook. Sharing a problem with a friend may be all we need to see it more clearly or let it go. Moving from busy physical activity to a few moments of quiet contemplation creates an inner balance. A problem that seems overwhelming at night may be met with new insight and new energy after a night's rest.

We don't have to continue feeling like victims of circumstance or remain stuck with a nagging problem. Just like changing the subject of a conversation, we can change the subject of our attention for a time. When we do, we regain our sense of hope and change our responses.

Today, I will give myself a break when I become caught or obsessed with a problem.

We must embrace the absurd and go beyond everything we have ever known.
                              —Janie Gustafson

We have stepped beyond the limits of our former life and accepted the possibility of the unknown. Many of us have always tried to be rational, to trust only what we could understand or reason through. That attempt served the part of us that lusted for control and power, but it kept us from unknown possibilities and dreams.

When we decide to be less controlling, we begin to believe in possibilities we didn't allow before. That is how we let God influence our lives. Perhaps we don't see a reasonable way to a more satisfying job, but we can be open to surprising possibilities. We may see nothing we can do to overcome our compulsions, but we pray for God to remove our shortcomings in God's way, and already we have a new attitude.

God, give me the courage to step into the unknown, the absurd, and experience the awakening of my spirit.

According to the teachers, there is only one thing that all people possess equally. This is their loneliness.

—Hyemeyohsts Storm

Many of us have tried to find a way to outwit our loneliness, or to escape its truth. We have learned that we cannot. As fathers looking at our children we may wish to spare them this pain. As men with our mates, we have dreamed of an ideal connection where all loneliness was dispelled.

We can't obliterate loneliness. But we can learn to accept and deal with it. There is no need to compulsively cover all traces and all reminders that we are alone. We can accept this universal truth. We are alone, but so is everybody. We can make true contact with each other out of our aloneness. True intimacy with another man or woman comes out of first seeing our separateness, and then bridging the gap.

Today, I accept the feeling of loneliness as part of life. I can make contact with my brothers and sisters, knowing we are all in the same condition.

I'd like to get away from earth awhile
And then come back to it and begin
again.

—Robert Frost

Do we think it's weak to need a break? Do we ignore the need to recharge our batteries? Responsibility for our own lives requires us to recognize the need to restore our energy. Maybe our former escape from the world was by using food, or drugs, or spending money, or sexual release, or preoccupation with another person.

Now, since we are developing the ability to be with ourselves, we can take a break from the world and come back restored. This meditation time generates more energy for our lives. Recreation with friends, a walk, a movie, or a concert does the same. Taking responsibility to get away is a good cure for self-pity and exhaustion.

Today, I will be aware of my need to restore my energy.

It is a terrible, an inexorable law that one cannot deny the humanity of another without diminishing one's own: in the face of one's victim, one sees oneself.

—*James Baldwin*

Acting totally in our self-interest is shortsighted and foolishly simple. Attacking another person or another nation reflects upon us like a mirror. When any person is undermined, the human race is diminished in some measure. And humanity is our family.

Sometimes we see a reflection of ourselves in someone else and fail to recognize it. What we hate most in another may well be what we are hating in ourselves. Knowing this can be useful. Perhaps our teeth are set on edge when we think about an ex-wife, or father, or former friend, or a religious or racial group. How are we like that person or group? What do they cause us to face within ourselves? When we stop diminishing the other person we may still not like him or her, but we can come to terms with ourselves. We learn to live and let live.

God, help me engage in the brotherhood of my own family and with all people—and to see my own face, even in my enemy.

There is overwhelming evidence that the higher the level of self-esteem, the more likely one will treat others with respect, kindness, and generosity. People who do not experience self-love have little or no capacity to love others.
—*Nathaniel Branden*

We cannot hang on to feelings of shame and guilt and still hope to become better people. How did these feelings begin? If we were treated badly by people, we need to be honest about what happened so we can resolve it and move on. Have we perpetuated our feelings by acting disrespectfully ourselves? Then we need to take a thorough inventory of our wrongdoings, admit them, make repairs, and let them go.

We may wallow in shame because facing it feels too frightening. Often, we believe our shame is greater than that of others. This belief is usually untrue and grandiose. It's part of how we isolate ourselves. We don't have to face it alone. We have the help of other men and women who can listen to our pain and tell us about their experiences.

Today, may I find the courage to face my shame and assert my right to self-esteem.

What I do today is important because I am exchanging a day of my life for it.
—*Hugh Mulligan*

We show self-respect in how we choose to spend our time. Do we give tasks the time required for our best efforts? Or do we feel unworthy of quality work? Do we have a right to stop working and just play? Are we worth spending time with—just ourselves, or do we feel meaningful time is only spent with others? Are we worth caring enough about to enjoy bathing, grooming, or getting haircuts? Do we care enough about ourselves to see a dentist or a physician when needed?

Choices about how we use our time are basic ethical and creative choices. Beyond self-respect and care, we need to put time into our day for nourishing and enriching our spirits. We do that by reading something thoughtful or meaningful, talking to a friend about the events and feelings of our lives, listening to music, fixing a pleasant meal, exercising, and giving unpaid time and energy to worthwhile causes.

I am grateful for the gift of another day, and I will live it creatively and respectfully.

A man's life is what his thoughts make it.
—*Marcus Aurelius*

How do we think about ourselves? Do we feel unattractive? Do we feel we aren't masculine enough? Do we doubt our ability to perform our roles as friends, husbands, or fathers? Such thoughts are common among men. There is no problem in having them; they are normal to some extent. But what we do with our thoughts—how we think about what we think—makes a big difference in our lives.

When we think we are odd or different from other men for feeling this way, we become more self-centered. When we don't stand up for our rights as men to have our doubts and weaknesses, we become even more weak and doubting. When we don't talk about our thoughts and feelings to other men, we become isolated and lonely. We have a right to feel insecure and to know we have weaknesses. We become stronger men by accepting our doubts. They may still cause some pain but they have lost their power to control us. Just as a repaired seam can be stronger than the original, what was our weakness becomes our strength.

Today, I accept my thoughts of weakness and self-doubt as part of life.

We did not all come over on the same ship, but
we were all in the same boat.
—Bernard M. Baruch

As we listen to others' stories and tell our own, we see roads into this program are different. Some of us hit bottom. Others were spared the worst catastrophes, getting the message of recovery early. In the final analysis, we are all in the same boat with our powerlessness. The differences are superficial. There is no higher or lower status for anyone in our program. When it comes to the power of our addictions and codependencies, we are equally in need of help from our Higher Power.

Perhaps there was a time when we felt totally alone with our problems. But we were alone just like thousands of others needing recovery. Because we all have suffered and know our need for help, we can now have a caring and supportive group. We can turn to our brothers and sisters in the program knowing that they are in the same boat, and they will understand. No one else provides that kind of healing relationship.

I am grateful for the closeness I have with others who are in the same boat with me.

Life is change . . .
Growth is optional . . .
Choose wisely . . .
                              —*Karen Kaiser Clark*

We can certainly count on change. We become fathers, our children become more independent, we make new friends, and other friends move away. When a man clings too tightly to the status quo or tries to control the direction of change, he is bound to be disappointed. We are like skiers on a mountain. We must continue down the slope. We can vary our speed somewhat, but if we stop for too long we will get cold or hungry; if we ski too fast, we may have a serious fall. Part of the pleasure is in not being able to control or predict every circumstance we will meet.

We don't control which loved ones come into our lives and which ones go or whether we become ill or stay healthy. We don't control life's opportunities. We can control how we choose to respond to these transitions. Whatever happens can be used for growth and we can commit ourselves to use all experiences that way.

Today, I will not try to control change but will choose to use whatever happens for growth.

The years forever fashion new dreams when old ones go. God pity the one-dream man.
—*Robert Goddard*

A painful loss can seem like the end of hope for us. It is true that the place a loved one had in our lives will never be filled. The loss of a job may dash a dream that will not come true—at least not as we thought it would. The aging of our body ends physical strength, and we lose options that will not come around a second time. Yet, change is a basic fact of life. We must empty a glass before we can fill it with something else. Our spiritual task is to become less rigid in our attachments and more accepting of the flow of life.

When we look straight at our losses and allow ourselves to cry and grieve over them, we are saying good-bye and letting go. Grief cleanses the soul and frees us to move on to new dreams. The loss of a job may put us in a position to discover undreamed of possibilities. In time, the loss of a love heals, and it deepens our relationship with our Higher Power and with our other friends. The other side of grief is freedom, and we are learning to have many new dreams in our lives.

I pray for the freedom that comes with having dreams in my life.

The most exhausting thing in life is being insincere.
—Anne Morrow Lindbergh

Many of us grew up in situations that required us to be constantly on our guard. We became so keenly attuned to the people around us and how to please them or avoid their anger that we lost contact with our inner messages. Rather than developing skills for drawing upon our inner resources, we developed skills for looking outward and reacting to whatever confronted us. This method of survival may have been necessary in the past while we were under stress, but it doesn't allow us any rest or the possibility of simply following what we know and feel is right.

We are learning to know what we think and feel and to express it, even if it isn't always what others want to hear. We can be spontaneous now because we have room for mistakes in our lives. Our relationships are more reliable, and we have more energy from sincerity than from always striving to make a good appearance.

Today, it is more important for me to be sincere than to be on my guard.

*Every human being is a problem in search of a
solution.*
                                        —*Ashley Montagu*

Each of us is a strong and fragile creature. We're always subject to forces outside our control, and we're learning steps for living that help us cope and rise above these problems. Our particular situation might seem special to us but in another sense, everyone's situation is a unique problem. Spiritual growth is the result of coming face-to-face with our own situation, feeling the brunt of our own puzzlement, recognizing no recipe will apply completely, and then trusting our Higher Power as we make unsure responses.

No school or parent can ever teach us enough to smooth our search for solutions. We become complete human beings by living through the muddle, by truly trusting our connections with God and other people to carry us along until we find clarity again. We progress into manhood when we meet our own particular life crises. We learn to see we have this process in common with every human being. Rather than resist our problems, we band together with others and pool our strength to find solutions.

My problems today are opportunities for spiritual growth.

Many situations can be clarified by the passing of time.
    —*Theodore Isaac Rubin*

Time heals our wounds. It teaches lessons that cannot be learned in a day. It allows truths to rise to the surface that first were difficult to see. In our impatience and restlessness we may forget that our answers come and our needs are often filled simply by waiting. We live in a goal-oriented world, and men are expected to go after what they want. But that is sometimes a foolish approach.

Our problems developed over time, and now recovery and growth take time. The learning we missed while we were absorbed in our excesses cannot be captured in a day. Anxieties and stresses come and go for everyone, but we often increased our problems by trying to cure what would pass on its own accord. We are learning to live more wisely through our periods of stress by trusting in the care of God.

Today, I will allow time to heal and correct rather than automatically reaching for a cure.

*The irony of your present eating habits is that
while you fear missing a meal, you aren't fully
aware of the meals you do eat.*
—Dan Millman

Many of us have had problems with eating. Some of
us eat compulsively. We may have become overly focused on diet or abused ourselves by mindlessly in-
dulging in unhealthy eating. We all grow by becoming
more aware of our relationship to food. Our spiritual
life is nourished by fully experiencing all our sensa-
tions concerning food.

We can begin with awareness of our empty stom-
achs and take pleasure in feeling hungry. We can give
time to eating and use a meal as a time for relationships. Taking pleasure in the preparation of healthy
food, making it look attractive, smelling the aromas,
tasting the flavors, and enjoying the fullness and renewed energy after eating are all ways of growing spiritually as we become healthier in our use of food.

---

*Today, I will take pleasure as I eat. I will make room in my
life for healthy nourishment of body and spirit.*

Just because a man lacks the use of his eyes doesn't mean he lacks vision.

—*Stevie Wonder*

It has been easy for many of us to meet our limitations with self-pity. Maybe we think being a real man means always being strong, capable, good-looking, and in charge. If we have a handicap, like blindness or a learning disability, we may have thought we were less masculine or less worthy.

All of us have handicaps. Some are greater than others, and some are more visible than others. These handicaps confront us with our powerlessness. We do not find our finest human qualities until we have met our limitations and accepted them. A new side of our strength develops when we accept our powerlessness and yield to it rather than trying to take charge of it. We develop greater vision when we stop feeling sorry for ourselves about our handicap and surrender to its truth. We then see our kinship with all men and women who struggle with their limitations.

Today, I will set aside self-pity and remember to be grateful for the lessons my limitations have taught me.

There is no greater weakness than stubbornness. If you cannot yield, if you cannot learn that there must be compromise in life—you lose.
—*Maxwell Maltz*

Glass is very hard, but fragile. By contrast, leather is tough and resilient. A blow to a glass dish will break it, but a blow to a shoe will just be absorbed. Our program leads us to avoid the folly of being hard like glass, and we become more tough like leather. We must endure surprises, pressures, and blows from the world as a normal part of life. The more able we are to absorb the blows, the stronger and more whole we are as men.

A friend who has a different opinion from ours can be listened to and his ideas considered. There is no need to compete with him or prove that we are right. When our plan for a project at work gets set aside, we will feel the frustration but we need not come apart over it. Perhaps our Higher Power is leading us to a better plan. Frustrations with spouses or friends can be turned over to our Higher Power. We do not have a rigid recipe for life, and we must be open to more learning.

I will surrender my fragile stubbornness in exchange for the toughness I can learn in compromise.

To know oneself, one should assert oneself.
—*Albert Camus*

We learn about ourselves by bumping up against something solid. By throwing ourselves into a project, meeting an obstacle we can't overcome, perhaps making some mistakes, we learn what we are capable of and what we are not. We are not here to live a comfortable and placid life. Our task is to grow and learn, to make a contribution, and to have some tranquility while we do. The only way we can achieve those goals is to assert ourselves, find out where the solid limits are, and assert our right to make mistakes in the process.

When we first learn to drive a car, we oversteer and hit the brakes too hard or too softly. In the process we learn how to feel what is just right. When we are learning to ask for what we need and to make a place for ourselves, we may ask too demandingly at times. That is not bad. It is how we will learn to do it well.

Today, I will have opportunities to assert myself. I will take the risks required to learn.

Lying to ourselves is more deeply ingrained than lying to others.

—Fyodor Dostoyevsky

The primary requirement for our recovery is honesty. In order to grow in honesty we first needed to see how we had lied to others and to ourselves. This was not as easy as it first appeared. Our lies to ourselves kept us so fully in the dark that we did not know we were lying. We sometimes told "sincere" lies because we honestly did not distinguish the truth within ourselves. For so long we had preferred dishonest rationalizations, and we had come to believe them.

The spiritual life of this program is based upon experience. What we feel, what we see and hear, is what we know. When we simplify our lives and base the truth upon our experiences, we slowly cleanse ourselves of the lies we told ourselves. With this kind of honesty comes an inner peace with ourselves in which we can say, "I know myself."

Today, I will accept my experience as a simple message of truth.

One cannot always be a hero, but one can always be a man.

—*Goethe*

In our all-or-nothing and grandiose lifestyles, many of us have had a lot of experience being heroes and being failures. Until we had achieved some sanity we didn't have much experience with being ordinary, genuine men. Many of us thought there was something fundamentally wrong with us. We tried to be great, and when we failed we felt less than human. Our shame in those experiences seemed to say we would never be normal again.

We are learning that being genuine is far more fulfilling than being great. We no longer have to swing between the opposite extremes of hero and coward. When we become honest with ourselves, we develop an internally respectful relationship with ourselves. That is when we become true men. The courage it has taken for us and others on this journey to become honest is heroic in the deepest sense of the word.

As I find the courage to be honest, I will become more genuine.

I am still learning.

— *Michelangelo's motto*

Is it okay for a man to say he does not know? Our myths of masculinity tell us we are supposed to know all about how to be great lovers, how to do a job, how to get from here to there. We should never look confused or bewildered because someone will think we are weak. This is certainly a boyish attitude! How can we ever learn anything new if we can't look like beginners? That's the way to be an underachiever. In our growing up, we can shed these small ideas and have the strength to admit we don't always know.

Many of us have had the experience of growing in years without growing more mature. Having a sponsor is one of the ways we can clearly arrange to be learners. We can also learn from the fellowship of other men and women in our group. To be learners, we need to be honest and straightforward about what we already know as well as about what we do not know. When we are willing to be learners, we grow emotionally.

I will be honest about things I don't know so I can continue to learn.

To be a man means to be a fellow man.
                                    —*Leo Baeck*

Sometimes we become overburdened with frustration and disappointment in our lives. When we turn inward and focus only on our problems, we may be cutting ourselves off from the healing effect of contact with others. Today, there may be a new group member who would appreciate a phone call from us. Perhaps we could visit an aged person or someone who is sick. Help is always needed in providing food to the hungry. Perhaps a co-worker would welcome our assistance on a task or errand.

When we help others, we affirm our solidarity with them in their stress and suffering. We don't give help because we are better or without problems of our own, but because we suffer too. When we act as fellowmen, the comradeship and human contact we get provide us with as much help as we give. They liberate us from our own oppressive egos and make us see we are worthwhile men.

I affirm myself as a man when I stand in solidarity with others and help them in their need.

Procrastination is the thief of time.
—Edward Young

When we have a problem with putting things off, we seem to add to our troubles by mentally flogging ourselves. We know we are losing time. We criticize ourselves for our irrational behavior. Whether we are putting off an important task in our lives or letting many little undone jobs accumulate, we could benefit from stopping the self-criticism and asking ourselves for the spiritual message in our actions. Perhaps we need some quiet time to do absolutely nothing. Maybe our perfectionism is paralyzing us. Is an "all-or-nothing" attitude telling us if we can't do the whole job right away, there is no point in beginning? Unexpressed anger may be blocking us from doing what we need to do.

Whenever we find ourselves doing things that seem irrational we can ask, "What is the message from my Higher Power in this behavior?" This question will carry us much further toward spiritual growth than the mental criticism we are tempted to do.

Today, I will do what I can within the limits of one day, and I will stay in communication with my Higher Power.

In the world to come they will not ask me, "Why were you not Moses?" They will ask me, "Why were you not Zusya?"

—*Zusya of Hanipoli*

We grow in the direction of the choices we make. That growth depends as much on *how* we make decisions as on *which* ones we make. Often in the past we tried to model ourselves after someone we admired. Our self-confidence was poor, so we depended on others to let us know if our decisions were correct, or we modeled our decisions on how we thought others would decide. Now we see that we can never become exactly like someone else and we need not try.

To each of us, God gives a creative task and a problem—to take our special abilities and limitations and become whole men. We use standards for our choices based on our best ideas of right and wrong, of what fits with our inner feelings, and of what our Higher Power is guiding us toward. Unfinished and imperfect as we are, we become more peaceful as we become more fully ourselves.

May I be true to myself in the choices I make today. I am becoming the man that I admire.

SEPTEMBER

If you wish to make an apple pie truly from scratch, you must first invent the universe.
—*Carl Sagan*

Everything is given to us. Our lives came forth with no plan on our part. We have no lease on life and no control, ultimately, over any possession. In the addictive and codependent families most of us came from, we learned something else. We learned a lonely arrogance that said, "I should be self-sufficient. I have earned everything that ever came to me." Deep down we probably knew how untrue that was, and we felt great self-doubt.

The cure we learn in this program for our lonely arrogance is a miracle and a blessing. We accept that we are part of a larger whole. Now it dawns on us—all of our friends and relatives share this basic powerlessness. We are all pilgrims. We are all guests. We are all stewards of creation. We can be close, and we must help one another because everyone is equally vulnerable.

I am grateful to my Higher Power today for the life which has been given me. I pray for greater understanding of my responsibilities.

A lot of what passes for depression these days is nothing more than a body saying that it needs work.

—Geoffrey Norman

Exercise changes our thought patterns in beneficial ways. Often we may feel irritable or blue and see nothing we can do about the situation. Then we are amazed at what simply going for a half-hour walk will do. Although our situations don't change, we are changed in how we respond to them. Exercise—whether going for a walk, working in the garden, playing ball, or scrubbing a floor—clears our minds. After some physical movement we find our thoughts getting more clear. Ideas come to mind that help us cope, and our spirit is energized.

Science has demonstrated that many serious cases of depression respond just as well to a program of vigorous daily exercise as to traditional treatment. In a sense, our Higher Power speaks to us through our muscles and bones when we move them. This spiritual experience, like many others, never comes from thinking about it, only from doing it.

Today, I will make time for physical activity.

It is clear the future holds opportunities—it also holds pitfalls. The trick will be to seize the opportunities, avoid the pitfalls, and get back home by 6:00.

—Woody Allen

Sometimes we take ourselves far too seriously. We draw our lives in the absolutes of black and white, with no shadings of gray. We believe our whole lives depend on every decision we make. When a problem comes along, we see it as a crisis rather than another of the ongoing issues that confront all people. If we are displeased with someone, or if a person is upset with us, we amplify the feelings until we rupture the whole relationship.

It would be helpful to look at today's tasks and problems as a game. Yes, we would like to play the game well, but we could have a good time while doing it. If we don't take ourselves or our problems too seriously, maybe we'll have some fun.

Help me learn that daily living needs the light of humor.

*It is as important to cultivate your silence power
as it is your word power.*

—William James

We bless ourselves with renewal and healing when
we retreat from the world for a few private moments of
silence. The power we cultivate in silence isn't gener-
ated by us; that power comes to us. We can do this by
deliberately withdrawing from all distractions. Then
we quiet our inner selves by concentrating on deep relaxation, thinking about a brief reading, or by praying.

Most of us already have a personal island of renewal
that we have turned to many times in the past for serenity and strength. We can use it and turn to it daily.
This natural pattern is necessary for a strong and
healthy life. It builds our relationship with ourselves
and our Higher Power. In our problems with self-
esteem, we often label as worthless the quiet, subtle
things we do, but these very things are essential to
build our strength and self-esteem.

*I will take time for silence to receive the power it gives in
my life.*

He brought me out into an open place; he rescued me because he delighted in me.
—*Psalms 18:19*

We know in this program that our recovery was not an accident. We may be mystified by it or surprised to be feeling better. Some of us call it a miracle. We have worked hard in our recovery. We have suffered through some difficulties. Yet, our recovery is not an achievement or an accomplishment. It is a gift from our Higher Power. We were powerless to help ourselves. All we could do was ask for help.

As we live an improved life and enjoy the benefits of our growth, we may ask why we were given this gift. As we seek to know the will of God, the ancient passage quoted today offers an answer. "He rescued me because He delighted in me." Can we let that in?

Thanks to God for all the rescued moments and for all the times I have been saved from my excesses.

I learned to listen to my body with an inner concentration like meditation, to get guidance as to when to exercise and when to rest. I learned that healing and cure are active processes in which I myself needed to participate.
—Rollo May

In our spiritual growth, one of our movements is from passive to active, from helpless to responsive. For example, we are passive if we don't take responsibility for our bodies and don't care for our wellness and conditioning. Do we passively leave our health in the doctor's hands?

Do we take responsibility for our relationships? Are we active in nurturing them? We could add our own interests and positive energy to enrich them.

Our Higher Power speaks to us in a quiet, subtle voice which can easily be ignored until we learn to listen. It takes courage to listen to this inner voice. When we listen, we develop a relationship that is a strong force moving us into recovery. We are still powerless over many things, but we can make active choices in how we will grow and how we will respond.

I will be guided in my choices by my inner voice.

Friendship and community are, first of all, inner qualities.

—*Henri J. M. Nouwen*

Many of us mistakenly search outside ourselves for answers. We feel small inside and not very powerful. Many of us men have tried to change our lives by affecting the people around us. Naturally, when we think of making friends, we assume we would start by getting a friend. But such beginnings often don't lead very far.

Friendship begins as an inward attitude or feeling before it is expressed outwardly. Perhaps we could first notice whom we feel friendly toward. Whom do we admire? Whom do we feel an affinity with? Let that friendliness exist within, and it will begin to express itself. Are we grasping for acceptance or response? Let us remain with our own goodwill and not return to old attempts to get someone else to change. Friendship exists as a feeling of admiration, of love, of fellowship, without demand. And when we are another man's friend, let us accept his friendship and enjoy it without trying to change it or him.

Today, I will simply notice my friendly feelings toward others.

It's hard for me to keep my emotions inside. I want to express them now. That's what a team is all about.

—Earvin "Magic" Johnson

We become part of a team in this program. That's why all the Steps are written with the word *we* rather than *I*. We cannot fully surrender to renewal simply by reading about it, hearing about it, or thinking about it. We become participants, members, and peers. We go to meetings and express the details of our lives, and we learn from the stories of others. In our relationships we learn to let our emotions out.

When we say, "He's hard to get to know," we are talking about someone who doesn't show feelings. Team members express their feelings to build a bond between themselves and gain a familiarity with each other. A man may say, "I'm the sort of guy who doesn't do well in groups," or "I'm not the type to express my feelings." But for the sake of recovery, we must endure the awkwardness of learning new things. On this recovery team it is all right to come just the way we are, awkwardness and all.

Today, I will not hold back my emotions. I will let people know me.

Don't let life discourage you; everyone who got where he is had to begin where he was.
—*R. L. Evans*

Feelings of discouragement are to be expected as part of life. We will have our times of greater energy and hope and our times of feeling depleted and lost. As we mature we learn to see many peaks and valleys across the landscape.

Giving ourselves over to feelings of discouragement is self-indulgent and saps our strength. We cannot see into the future. The dailiness of our lives isn't always dramatic and doesn't usually offer great changes. But we are part of an unfolding process. Looking back over just a week or a month, we can recall troubled times that now seem insignificant. We see other people and their progress, and we know they too grew just one day at a time and couldn't see what the future would bring them. So we continue—knowing that our process is hopeful—even though we cannot foresee the details of our future.

I have the strength to live through the peaks and valleys and to stay faithful to my recovery.

It is not a question of how a husband and wife can be equal and alike. But rather, it is a problem of how a couple can be equal and different.

—*Pierre Mornell*

In seeking closeness with loved ones, we have often made the mistake of looking only for similarities. Although common ground helps understanding, we must learn how to get close to others by "borrowing their eyes and ears." We expand our understanding of others by accepting that what we see, hear, think, and feel will not be exactly what anyone else does. We can deepen our relationships by exchanging our experiences with others.

We don't have to agree on everything. Simply learning about each other's differences and letting each other know that we hear and understand will create a feeling of intimacy.

I will be receptive and appreciate differences in those I love.

A man can stand a lot as long as he can stand himself.

—*Axel Munthe*

Sometimes we're mistaken about the source of our unhappiness. We walk around with a short fuse, ready to explode if anyone crosses our path. Then, when we do explode, we think it is the other person's fault. At other times we have frightening physical reactions and worry that something is wrong with our bodies. But we are not aware that the problem is caused by a deeper feeling of not being able to stand ourselves.

Most of us have problems accepting ourselves. When we make peace with our consciences, some of our problems vanish. Other problems may never disappear, but our pain is eased because our inner battle has ceased and we have the energy we need to cope.

I am grateful for the gift of self-respect this program gives me.

*Not all fights are bad, in fact they are preferable
to disciplined serenity.*

—William Atwood

A good relationship includes some disagreement.
Anger and disagreement, when we express them respectfully, are important ways of renewing communication and breaking through the walls that sometimes
build up. No relationship can tolerate constant fighting. But, when we don't agree with someone, we owe
it to that person to speak up and follow through to
resolution. We can promise ourselves and the other
person that we will stay in the relationship through
the disagreement. It is because we care that we fight.

In any relationship we care about, there will be differences. When we avoid all confrontations, our relationships go stale because all emotional issues are
avoided. Carefulness and overcontrol undermine love
because they don't give it room to breathe, but disagreement and anger expressed in honest and respectful ways will help love grow.

*Today, I pray for the courage to acknowledge my
disagreements and angry feelings with others and to deal
with their feelings toward me.*

Mothers give sons permission to be a prince but the father must show him how. . . . Fathers give daughters permission to be princesses. And mothers must show them how. Otherwise, both boys and girls will grow up and always see themselves as frogs.

—Eric Berne

Relationships with our fathers have been central in shaping our characters. We catch ourselves saying what we heard our fathers say, or doing something we know they did. Many of us have had pain and resentments in these relationships. We wanted more time than they gave us, or we longed for praise but got criticism, or we were never sure we measured up to them.

Some of us can change our relationships with our fathers. We can do it, not by asking them to be different, but by being our full adult selves with them. This new experience is the doorway to a new aspect of our selves. Many of us cannot change our relationships with our fathers, but being with our sons and daughters in ways that nurture their growth is another chance to redo for ourselves what we missed.

My father's importance to me is a fact I must surrender to. I will take what he has given me and grow with it.

When a person drowns himself in negative thinking he is committing an unspeakable crime against himself.

—Maxwell Maltz

Negative thoughts can rule our lives as compulsively as an addiction. The feelings of power we get from holding a dismal and gloomy outlook deprive us of the positive and pleasant parts of life. Some of us have said, "If I expect the worst, I won't be disappointed. If I think the worst about myself, no one else can cut me down." It is like taking a driving trip and looking only for trash and garbage in the ditches, ignoring the beauty beyond. Indeed, what we see may be real, but it is a very limited piece of the picture.

When we have relied on negative thinking, it feels risky to give it up. We cannot do it in one day. We can begin by imagining ourselves with a more open attitude toward ourselves and the world. Then we can try it out as an experiment in little ways, with no commitment. Finally we reach the point where we can take a risk and entrust our Higher Power with the outcome.

Today, I will experiment with hopeful and positive thoughts about what happens.

When people are loving, brave, truthful, charitable, God is present.
                                        —*Harold Kushner*

For many of us, our spiritual awakening began when we first heard our Higher Power might be our group. We learned that God may exist in the connections between people in our group just as well as within each individual. As we members exchange care and help with each other, as each struggles to achieve complete honesty and wrestles bravely with old temptations, God is truly in our midst. Closeness flourishes because we felt so alone but then found friends who suffered in similar ways. It is an expression of a spirit beyond our rational control.

When we ask another member to listen to us, we contribute to the strength of this spirit. When we give someone a ride to a meeting or spread the word about this program to other suffering men and women, we make a contribution and receive its benefits. Even now, if we need a renewal of confidence in God's presence in our lives, we can telephone another member and just talk. We will quickly sense the spirit.

Today, I am grateful to feel God's presence in my life and within the people around me.

Sit loosely in the saddle of life.
—*Robert Louis Stevenson*

Sitting loosely in the saddle is an image of detachment for us. Detachment doesn't mean we stop caring. It means we have an inner wisdom telling us what we can control and what we cannot. When we go to meetings and hear fellow members struggling with temptations to return to old behaviors, we need to detach. When family members or friends are engaged in an addiction, we need to sit loosely in the saddle by caring, but not protecting them from the results of their behavior. Sometimes close friends will be "off base" in the way they talk to us. We practice detachment by not being reactive to the person but being responsive to the inner message of what kind of men we wish to be.

We can't control another person's behavior toward us. Our inner security will never come from how someone else behaves. The most helpful thing we can do for someone is to listen and care; then we need to be ready to let go of the outcome.

I will accept the limits of my control over others. I will care and let go.

Self-love, my liege, is not so vile a sin as self-neglecting.
—*William Shakespeare*

An important part of our lives is simply tending to our basic needs—sitting down daily to share a meal with loved ones, getting enough sleep, setting time aside for haircuts and polishing shoes, spending leisure time with friends. Paying attention to these things only when they become crises makes our lives unbalanced and crisis-oriented. Many men have neglected themselves because they felt it was the mark of a tough guy. Others have been so lost in an addiction or so codependent that a respectful self-caring life was not possible.

As we regain our sanity, we find balance in the basics. Self-love allows us to be responsible for our care, and it puts us in a stronger position to help others, to be creative, and to assert our right to recovery.

Today, I will look after the essentials of my personal care and my family's care before I take on other things.

Grace strikes us when we are in great pain and restlessness. It strikes us when we walk through the dark valley of a meaningless and empty life.
—Paul Tillich

We are men who know the consequences of alcoholism, codependency, and addiction. We have walked dark valleys. We have felt meaningless and empty in our lives. Each of us has a story. The harder we worked to overcome those feelings by our individual efforts, the worse the feelings got. This program suggested we try something radically new—something we couldn't think up on our own.

Grace is the love and generosity of God which comes through no effort of our own. Not until we felt defeated would we open ourselves to this gift of help from our Higher Power. Grace comes in many forms. It is in the hope we feel in the morning after a night of rest, and it's in the good feeling we get attending our meetings. Before this program, most of us were trying so hard to control our lives we couldn't notice any gifts that came from outside our efforts. These Twelve Steps train us for becoming receptive to the healing grace of God.

The grace of God surrounds me—even in difficult times. Returning to that message renews my strength.

Who's not sat tense before his own heart's curtain?
— *Rainer Maria Rilke*

Meeting ourselves and our Higher Power is the universal spiritual process. Sitting before the curtain of our hearts may feel as awesome to us or as frightening as anything we will ever do. When we first admit to ourselves a deeper truth, we feel these overpowering tensions. For some of us, this is a necessary step which leads to self-knowledge and inner peace. We feel unique, different, alone, maybe even crazy. For the first time, we are listening to our inner truth rather than outside messages.

Let's think for a moment about today's tensions and strains. Are we really aware of their source? Perhaps they are created by the disturbing honesty of our hearts? We may find our spiritual growth in yielding to the truth. When we are cynical about spiritual experience or when we minimize the importance of our soft-spoken inner wisdom, we are avoiding the truth from our hearts. And we miss the possibility of becoming strong from within.

Today, I will live through the tension and fear of my honesty to reach the point of peace with myself.

Sexuality expresses God's intention that people find authentic humanness not in isolation but in relationship.

—James B. Nelson

We men have regarded our sex lives and our spiritual lives as two different worlds. This attitude has caused many crises—anger and frustration with our partners, power struggles, accusations and hurt feelings, shame and guilt about our own behavior.

We can join our spirituality with our sexual selves by taking responsibility for being sexual. Being responsible means we take the risk of being vulnerable, of giving and receiving affection and sexual expression in our relationships. We cannot expect satisfaction of our desires simply because we feel them. In sexuality, as in all parts of our lives, our Higher Power is our guide. We can also say no to sexual expression if we wish.

God guide my sexual awareness today. Open me to experience sexuality as a creative gift for relationships.

He underwent a nine-and-a-half-hour opera-
tion. On the eighth day his wife picked him up
from the hospital and said, "You want to go
home?" to which he replied, "No, I want to go to
the office."

— *Herb Goldberg*

What is it that drives us men to such extremes in
our work? Are we afraid of the intimacy we could develop with those who love us and whom we love? Are
we driven to prove over and over that some old painful self-doubt is untrue? Is this how we feel masculine? Or are we trying to control our addictive
problems by constant work? Perhaps we still have
more to learn about surrender and powerlessness.

It is especially common to recovering men that the
excesses of addiction and codependency get unconsciously replaced by the excesses of work. This too is
an unhealthy escape. We must confront our relationship to work if we are to continue on our path of spiritual awakening. It is good to have some unplanned,
unstructured time in each day.

Today, help me remember that being good at my work is
only one of my qualities.

Time never challenged the Indian or worked against him. Time was for silently marking the passing of the seasons. It was a thing to be enjoyed.

—Tim Giago

We have a choice as to how we view the passage of time. We can look at it as a gift to be enjoyed, marking the transitions and cycles of life. Or we can think of time as a long, thin string of pressures and frustrations—specific minutes and hours that we try to speed up or slow down. Our relationship to time is a very important part of our recovery.

We are learning to live in the present, one day at a time. We are letting go of the past. The future we place in trust to our Higher Power. Time doesn't work against us or challenge us, it just flows. This day need not be painless or close to paradise for us to live in the present moment. Being aware of our lives without struggling against time makes the day rich and full of meaning.

Today, rather than wrestling with time, I will be aware of my experiences and let time flow.

Granted that I must die, how shall I live?
                                            —Michael Novak

On our recovery path we sometimes fall into a hole. As we get more in touch with ourselves and with reality, we might be overwhelmed, frightened, or depressed. Many men have asked, "How can it be that I live life with such struggle and hard work only to die in the end?" In recovery we no longer have our anesthetic, our drug of choice, our excesses and controlling behaviors to dull this painful awareness.

Growing as a human being means becoming more aware of these dark truths and not being paralyzed by them. We accept death and choose life. That means we live fully in the present. We choose relationships with others. We appreciate the beauty of creation and seek to know the will of God. In recovery, we choose to live this day fully, in contact with friends and loved ones, appreciating the beauty around us, and helping those we can.

God, help me to tune in to your truth, and to be a living part of your constant creative process.

Life is painting a picture, not doing a sum.
                                            —Oliver Wendell Holmes, Jr.

As we go about our activities, we will have a richer day when we think of ourselves as painting a picture instead of keeping score. Rather than woodenly completing a task, we might approach it as something that can be made interesting. Instead of driving to work or riding the bus only to reach our destination, we might think of this routine as part of the picture we paint today. When a friend makes a comment, we might think of it as another brush stroke in our painting and join in with him, rather than making a game or contest which we must try to win.

Many of us men were taught that success means having the highest score. So we have become compulsively competitive—always trying to be right, always striving for more financial security, or always pushing ourselves for some new achievement. Success may not be coming out on top. When our lives are lived as rich and interesting pictures, we find our rewards are far deeper and more lasting.

May the picture I paint today be one I will carry with me and appreciate.

Be thine own palace, or the world's thy jail.
—*John Donne*

All of us have some difficult circumstances to face today. Some among us find ourselves in the hospital or in jail. Others are worried about pressures and frustrations at work. Tensions and concerns about war and the future of the world affect us all. We have many uncontrollable circumstances in our lives, but we don't have to give ourselves over to them. A man's body may be in jail while in his heart he is free.

We build a palace for our spirits by maintaining contact with our Higher Power. We are always within the circle of God's love. Always! Knowing that helps us make peace with the limits on what we can do about our situations. Then we can go forth working to make peace in our relationships, accomplish what is possible in our lives, and make a contribution to others.

Today, I will remember that the frustrations around me are not all of who I am. When I am at peace within, I live among spiritual riches.

To try to extinguish the drive for riches with money is like trying to quench a fire by pouring butterfat over it.

—*Hindu proverb*

In recovery, we learn what we truly want and what is only a symbol of our desires. Do we truly want to use our energies pursuing success, or are we seeking approval from others? Do we truly want money so much, or are we attempting to escape the basically insecure nature of life? Do we truly enjoy the pleasure of food so much, or are we in search of comfort for our emotions?

Our desires, our wants, and our anxieties are spiritual issues. What at first we think we want may only hide deeper, more vulnerable, and painful feelings. When we admit the deeper fears and desires, we move closer to the spiritual truths of our lives. We can search for acceptance within ourselves and from God. We can learn to have spiritual peace in an insecure world. We can learn to accept the love of others even though we know we're not perfect.

Today, I will ask myself what I want and listen with courage to my answer. It will lead me in my spiritual progress.

What I have wanted is consistency, ever since the day back in Wyncote when my mom and dad split. I have wanted to be liked. I have wanted to be loved. I have wanted to be in a family-type atmosphere.

—*Reggie Jackson*

How many of us gave ourselves away trying to fix painful childhood longings? We thought if we were good boys, good men, caretakers, we would have the love we wanted. Sadly, our remedies for childhood pain have often been childish solutions. Our need for security may have become a self-centered obsession and blocked our ability to hear our loved ones. We may have become so fervent about accepting others that we failed to stand up for ourselves and lost their respect.

Most of us reach adulthood with leftover pain no person could ever fix. We learn grown-up responses by accepting our load of pain and by asking others for help. Intimacy and companionship reduce the weight. We tell our friends about our burdens, and we learn what they are carrying. In the process we grow in wisdom and maturity.

Today, I will remember I do not have to be alone with my pain.

Life itself is the proper binge.

—*Julia Child*

The Twelve Steps are a suggested program of recovery, not a cure. We can follow them and live a healed life, but we never develop immunity to our addictions and codependency. We remain vulnerable to slips, binges, and a return to old behaviors. If that has happened to us, our first need is to find a way back to the program. A slip may speak the blatant truth we avoided before. A man's complete honesty following a slip has sometimes been the way to renewed knowledge of his powerlessness. There is no value in feeling more shame and self-hate in the aftermath of a slip. We need to accept we are incomplete and imperfect human beings. Recovery will come, not from shame, but from honestly accepting our powerlessness and the help we need.

The promise of recovery in this program, a healed life, is just as available after a slip as it ever was. It takes absolute commitment, a willingness to face the pain and hardship. Then we are freed again to engage fully in the joy and the awe of life.

I ask that my compulsions and my weaknesses be lifted from me. I'm not able to cure myself, but I pray for help.

Life without idealism is empty indeed. We must have hope or starve to death.

—*Pearl Buck*

Our ideals, the principles that order our lives, are essential to a healing life. Some of us have lived a pattern in which we did not know what we believed. If someone we liked stated a viewpoint, we might wear it for a while like a new shirt—but with no personal commitment. Others of us have indulged in negativism and hopelessness. Life is more fulfilling when we assert our beliefs and give ourselves to them. As human beings, we are unable to perfectly live out our beliefs, but we become whole men by giving our energies to the attempt.

Is beauty in music, art, and nature a worthwhile ideal for us? Are fairness and justice for all people what we value? Are love and brotherhood ideals we hold dear? When we dare assert these values in our lives, they are life-giving to us. They mature us. Reaching for what is worthwhile, rather than cursing what is not, gives us a design for making all our choices, and we have hope.

I will dare to meet my negativism with my ideals. My spiritual health will give me life.

The man who never alters his opinion is like standing water, and breeds reptiles of the mind.
—William Blake

We seek *the answer*. Sometimes we think we have found a central truth and later learn that beneath it is another truth. Or what seemed so crucial as a guiding principle for our lives last year is still true but not as crucial. It is like trying to take a snapshot of a changing world while the camera itself is changing.

Some of us in our hunger for security grab for "absolute" truths which are not absolute. We must continue forever to be eager learners. In stepping across a stream from one floating log to another, we must resist the temptation to become overcommitted to staying in an especially secure-looking place, or we will never reach the opposite shore. Even the Twelve Steps of this program are given to us as a "suggested" program of recovery. It is a program that works because it takes us out of our rigid ways. We are continually made new. That is the vitality of the spiritual life.

God, help me to be open to new opinions—to things I had never thought of on my own.

OCTOBER

It was football time, apple time, harvest time, hunting time, school time. Footsteps quickened. It was exciting to be in transition. It seemed more like the beginning of something than like the end of it.

—Paul Gruchow

Some days seem filled with the exciting energy of change. They are like walking on a bridge from one time period to the next. In the fall, our senses are filled with messages of change. Trees tell us it is happening. So do football games, and the cool chill in the morning air.

As summer wanes and winter approaches, we may need to grieve for what we leave behind before greeting what comes next. The changes we experience in recovery bring similar responses. We grieve the loss of our old friends, the bottle, the food binge, the romantic thrill, or the excitement of gambling or spending. We are able to grieve our losses because we accept them. We have chosen them. Now we move to the next season of our lives.

As I experience the circle of seasons outside me, I am grateful for the ongoing flow of change within.

*One ought, each day at least, to hear a little
song, read a good poem, see a fine picture and, if
possible, speak a few reasonable words.*
　　　　　　　　　　　　　　　　—Goethe

A spiritual man can nourish his growing spirit
through enriching and beautiful experiences. Such experiences might be quiet meditation, reading something which provides ideas to ponder, conversation
with a friend, or listening to music. Men have been
taught to focus on things more than on people, on
goals and achievement, and we neglect to provide ourselves with nourishment for our minds and souls.

Life's experiences include joy and beauty and pain
and grief. If we are uplifted every day by beauty in its
many forms, we are strengthened and carried along to
meet the tougher parts of our day. We may need to
push some other things aside to have it. Perhaps some
jobs can wait until tomorrow, and we can linger over a
meal with our loved ones. Maybe mowing the lawn or
fixing the car isn't as important as a half hour of good
music. Do we make space for nourishing moments in
each day?

---

*I am grateful for the beauty all around. Help me keep life
more balanced so I can receive the spiritual nourishment it
provides.*

You should not have your own idea when you listen to someone. . . . To have nothing in your mind is naturalness. Then you will understand what he says.

—Shunryu Suzuki

A man who is mistrustful and self-centered has difficulty listening to someone else. Perhaps a woman we are close to wants to be understood by us. But we do not hear her on her own terms because we are so intensely involved with our own shame. So we react to our feelings of guilt rather than really hearing what she wants to say about her experience. Or we may be so worried about who has control that we fail to receive the information we are being given. Then we respond with "Yes, but . . ."

True learning comes—like true intimacy—when we have an open mind. As we detach ourselves, separate from our own ego, we hear the other person better and grow more intimate.

May I learn to set aside my own self-centeredness. Today, I will grow more if I set my ego aside when others are talking to me.

Anxiety is that range of distress which attends willing what cannot be willed.
— *Leslie H. Farber*

There are hundreds of ways in which men try to will things that cannot be willed. We will to sleep; we will to have others like us; we will to have sexual virility. In all these things, the force of our will does not work because what we want is not controllable. They come to us as an outcome of many factors—when the situation is right—when we have become ready for them.

When we could not let go, when we did not know how to turn our life and our will over to the care of God, we became more and more anxious. Then we turned to our addictive or codependent escapes from anxiety and willfulness. It is the folly of our age to try to take charge of everything. We are following a more peaceful and more successful way. We are doing our part and receiving the benefits that come to us.

The will of my Higher Power has a loving purpose and is far wiser than I.

Men are doomed to live in an overwhelmingly tragic and demonic world.
—*Ernest Becker*

Life is difficult. We never reach the point where our path is free of obstacles and hardships. And regardless of how much we grow, how faithful we are to our program, nothing changes the fact that death is still there for us. As painful and hard as it is, life also is deeply meaningful and worthwhile when we submit to its reality and live in a spiritual way.

After we stop living in denial and accept the hard facts about life, we see that we need each other. We need relationships to stay sane. We need to pull together and support one another the way people do in difficult times. Rugged individualism isn't always good for real people in the real world. We need relationships so we can celebrate and make music and encourage one another. We need relationships so we can laugh and make jokes and tell our personal stories. And we need to stand together to oppose the destructive forces around us.

God help me learn to have relationships with my brothers and sisters.

Forgiveness is another word for letting go.
—Matthew Fox

Learning forgiveness—both granting it to others and accepting it for ourselves—is one of the primary means of a man's spiritual recovery. Many of us, after entering this program, are plagued with strong feelings of guilt. We have finally become accountable, and we see our lives in a new perspective. We long for a chance to undo our mistakes. Many men carry guilt for years as if they deserved to be punished. Our recovery program tells us to let go.

Simply going through the motions of forgiving or accepting forgiveness will not get us very far. We must squarely face our feelings and tell someone so we are no longer alone with our guilt. Then, if there is the possibility for repair without further hurt, we must make repair. In this concrete way we can be genuinely forgiven and fully accept forgiveness. When a man has a spiritual experience like this, he matures and gains the ability to forgive others.

I am grateful for the relief of being forgiven and letting go of past mistakes. I will genuinely let go of my guilt and resentment.

If there are two hundred people in a room and one of them doesn't like me, I've got to get out.
—Marlon Brando

How much acceptance is enough for us? Do we feel one person's criticism undermines the acceptance of 199 others? Do we get so focused on one person's negative response to us that we cannot hear the positive? If we are unable to accept criticism from others, it becomes a sink without a plug, draining away all the positives we naturally have in our life.

As we become spiritual men, we're able to detach from negative and critical messages. We must still hear them. We must still listen to their messages because we can learn from them. But we can separate ourselves from the negative message. We can make a mistake. We can be disliked by someone. But we do not give up our places as equal, worthwhile men for any reason.

God, I pray for your support when my own strength to stand up for myself falters.

We cannot avoid
Using power,
Cannot escape the compulsion
To afflict the world,
So let us, cautious in diction
And mighty in contradiction,
Love powerfully.

—Martin Buber

The use and misuse of power by men give us much to weep over and much to admire. In our own families we see how our parents fought over power, how they used it both wisely and abusively. Our problems with power and control are a central part of our addictions and codependency. Admitting our powerlessness has started us toward recovery. Admitting our power will help carry us further.

No one is innocent beyond childhood. We affect the people around us, and it matters how we treat them. We cannot come and go unnoticed. Since we will make an impact, we learn to treat ourselves and the people around us with respect and justice. Our only solution is to learn to love and be loved.

Today, I will be more aware of the power I have in others' lives.

Nothing worse could happen to one than to be completely understood.

—Carl Jung

We so often long to be understood. We imagine it would cure our loneliness and empty feelings. We think of it as a kind of intimacy. Yet, we may be longing for a false goal. We are each a unique man on an incomplete journey. We don't yet fully understand ourselves. There is still much mystery beneath the surface of our being. If our partners or friends completely understood us, where would we go from there? We would no longer belong to ourselves.

Perhaps we are completely understood by our Higher Power but not by another person. It is a fact of life that we continue to grow and to reveal deeper layers of ourselves. We have relationships in which we can share the mysteries as they unfold. We can talk and be understood. In communication we find our closeness and intimacy.

Today, I will remember that at the deepest level no one can fully understand me. I will communicate with others to deal with my loneliness.

The last of the human freedoms is to choose one's attitudes.

—*Victor Frankl*

When we stand and look at a mountain, it looks awesome, majestic, and perhaps intimidating. To climb the mountain we will need to select a route. Which approach will give us success? Which will provide a beautiful view? Which is safest? What are the rewards and trade-offs among the paths available?

In our lives, we usually cannot choose the mountains that face us, but we can choose the best paths to approach them. One path may be a very negative attitude. It may feel safe like a narrow, protected passageway. It is predictable, but it keeps us cut·off from others. Another path may be filled with too many self-indulgent pleasures and never progress in any direction. Another path may be hard and include some risks, but it allows us to be in contact with others and to appreciate the beauty along the way. When we make positive choices about our attitudes, although the mountain is challenging, we are liberated to become the kind of men we're meant to be.

Today, I will choose friendly attitudes toward myself that will help me on my journey.

What is most beautiful in virile men is something feminine; what is most beautiful in feminine women is something masculine.
—*Susan Sontag*

In recovery, we grow in many ways and become more comfortable with the many subtle colors in our personalities. We have a greater range of all human qualities available to us now. We are more light and playful at times and more serious at others. We can cuddle up like a dependent child, or we can be the one who is responsible under pressure. We can be tough and virile, and we can be soft and gentle. One musical tone playing in harmony with another makes a song more beautiful. Because we have made peace within ourselves, our masculinity is not threatened.

As we discover many new feelings and reactions, it is natural to wonder if they are normal. When we talk with others about the ways we have changed, we learn they have similar feelings. As we become more at peace with ourselves, the various sides of our personalities complement each other, and we appreciate the harmony within us and in our friends.

Today, I am grateful for the richness and variety within myself.

I resolve to meet evil courageously, but when even a small temptation cometh, I am in sore straits. That which seemeth trifling sometimes giveth rise to a grievous temptation.
—*Thomas à Kempis*

Even in recovery, we know we are vulnerable men, always subject to a return to old patterns. Sometimes we can understand the triggering event, other times there is no apparent reason for temptation to reappear. Perhaps it comes when we least expect it, when our guard is lowest. We may be tempted simply because we are addicts or codependents. Our powerlessness reminds us of our need for faithfulness to the program.

When we think we have moved beyond the draw of old behaviors, we veer away from our path of recovery. In saying we have grown out of our powerlessness, or that our resolve can now protect us, we are heading back into old troubles. Admitting the truth is unsettling. It also makes us more honest, more accessible, more spiritual, and readier to deal with threats to our recovery.

I live with my powerlessness every day. Help me admit it to myself.

I can sing a prayer as well as say it.
—*Baal Shem Tov*

Lightness of spirit, song, and liberation are the products of a hearty spirituality. There is never a moment we don't have reason to fret or mourn. If we need to grieve, our recovery helps and supports us. But more than that, we are freed in this new life to be men of song and humor. We can sing although life is painful, because we are part of a group of recovering people. We're part of an unfolding mystery. We have love and it is beautiful.

Each time we let go of a secret or an old guilt or a worry about the future, our spirit is lightened. Maybe we experience this at its fullest while spending time with friends who take us just as we are. Perhaps we find it by seeing a funny movie or singing with a group. In the wisdom of the Steps, we are asked to do difficult and painful tasks which lead to our spiritual awakening. A light spirit celebrates the outcome of our hard work.

I will remember that my laughter and song are also ways of praying.

No man is more cheated than the selfish man.
—Henry Ward Beecher

When we're selfish, we close off the channels of exchange with others. Not only are we grabbing and holding all the goods or attention we can get, but we are denying others the possibility of sharing with us in the benefits. We may be selfish in material goods, but there are many other ways too. Some of us expect our spouses to meet our needs while we make little effort to meet theirs. Some of us discover our selfishness as we drive, refusing to yield a position to another car or getting furious if we lose a place in heavy traffic.

By contrast, our generosity and welcoming responses nourish the spirit within us and create a good environment for our growth. Sometimes giving does not come easily. We have a more generous spirit when we are in touch with our ultimate vulnerability. All of life is fragile, and we need each other to have a good life. We can truly hold onto nothing but ourselves. Giving what we can of our time, our energy, and our goods, helps create the kind of world we want to live in.

Today, I will look for ways to be generous with those I share this world with.

We know about remorse and death. But do we know about hope and life? I believe in life after birth!

—Maxie Dunham

We do not need to create difficulties and pain in our lives. They come with the package of human existence. Some of us even feel bewildered when we aren't pressed by trouble. As we grew in recovery and our lives became better ordered, many of us thought, "Life seems to be going so well; I wonder what's wrong?" We were more accustomed to remorse and crisis than to joy and serenity.

What lies before us today is an unpainted picture. There are many possibilities for events to take a good turn. This, too, is part of the package, but we must believe and affirm the good things in order to accept them. When our only expectations are pain and trouble, they probably will be our only experiences. However, when we have faith that a better life is possible, we open ourselves to receive it.

Today, I will live with hope for the possibilities and accept the good things that come my way.

One of the main reasons wealth makes people unhappy is that it gives them too much control over what they experience. They try to translate their own fantasies into reality instead of tasting what reality itself has to offer.

—Philip Slater

We are constantly told that the way to happiness is through material possessions. "Men who drive this sports car have all the women after them!" "If I could only own this special tool it would make me happy!" What does a man really want? He wants a feeling that his life makes sense. He wants the give-and-take of loving relationships. He wants to feel he has a place in the world and can make a contribution. And he wants the feeling that he is not standing still, but growing in those ways.

Being poor certainly limits our options, but material wealth is an empty seduction. Putting all our energies into capturing wealth may make us rich, but it also can become an addiction that causes unhappiness. We become much richer in our souls and in our experiences when we take the risks that help us improve our relationships and teach us how to live balanced lives.

I will live each moment in ways that fit my true values.

I never suspected that I would have to learn how to live—that there were specific disciplines and ways of seeing the world I had to master before I could awaken to a simple happy, uncomplicated life.

—Dan Millman

Wisdom begins in seeing how much we do not know. Sometimes it's a painful blow to our egos to face what we still have to learn. Many of us have believed we know how to live. Yet, when we look at our lives, we see something has been missing. When we continue to have great stress, when we haven't made progress in simplifying our lives, when our lives seem full of crises—perhaps then it is time to open ourselves to some new learning.

We can talk to sponsors and get ideas from group members. Perhaps they have noticed our blind spots and will tell us if asked. Expressing our problems in specific ways may point us to new learning. Our program teaches us twelve specific disciplines for our growth. We need to return to them again and again. We can always ask ourselves, "What Step am I working on at this time?" We may need to learn new ways to work on a specific Step.

I will turn to my fellow group members and focus on one Step for my growth today.

Thou art everywhere, but I worship you here;
Thou art without form, but I worship you in
*   these forms;*
Thou needest no praise, yet I offer you these
*   prayers and salutations.*

—Hindu prayer

The history of the Twelve Steps tells us that in the first small A.A. group there was controversy about the word God. For some of the men God was known in traditional religious ways; other members were agnostic. This first group followed their group conscience. The resolution they achieved has inspired many new Twelve Step members ever since. They were guided through their disagreement to a new expression of their spiritual relationship. They began to speak of a "Power greater than ourselves" and of "God, as we understood Him."

Today we turn to God as we understand God, because our definitions are restricted by human limitations. We know from our own experiences and from the stories of thousands of men and women who have preceded us, that this spiritual program is very practical and simple. It works. It restores our lives.

To a Power greater than myself, I am filled with gratitude.

If only I could throw away the urge to trace my patterns in your heart I could really see you.
—David Brandon

Trying to control and change the people around us creates great problems in our relationships. When people we love are expressing themselves, we're thinking about what we wish they would say, and it blocks us from hearing clearly. A need for safety and for a guarantee that we won't be abandoned urges us to manipulate the people we love. We know we have innocent motives. We say we only want what is best and that we are only trying to protect ourselves or be helpful. But we hide from the effects our actions have on our relationships.

We seem to be more trapped in these self-centered behaviors with the ones we are closest to. We can change ourselves by slowly releasing our security grip on others. We can focus more on understanding what others are saying to us than on changing how they think and feel. Intimacy is clearly seeing each other and knowing the differences as well as the similarities. It requires that both people be allowed to walk on separate paths.

I will release my grip on my loved ones and turn to my Higher Power for security and serenity.

Life is not a spectacle or a feast; it is a predicament.

—*George Santayana*

We could probably feel more tranquil if the world were a simpler place and always gave us simple answers. But we are faced with many ambiguous and uncertain situations. The changing roles of men and women can often leave us bewildered. We are engaged in the development of relationships that have lives of their own, and it's not always clear where they are headed. Even within ourselves we have contradictory feelings, and it's difficult to come up with clear answers.

Since we cannot force simplicity upon the world, we must turn to ourselves for a new response. We can become more tolerant of our unsettled predicaments. We can learn to have faith that good comes from change. Things have a way of settling out and clarifying with time. As we develop patience with the questions and the unclear issues in our lives, we gain a deeper serenity.

Today, I will recall the predicaments in my past life that, in time, became clearer, and I will have patience with what seems unsettled.

No man can produce great things who is not thoroughly sincere in dealing with himself.
—*James Russell Lowell*

We are in the business of producing miracles. The renewal of life in us and others in this program is a great event and happens only after we establish an honest relationship with ourselves. No longer can we excuse our minimizing and little white lies that push aside the truth. No longer can we deny our private fears and self-doubts. In our growing sincerity with ourselves, we can admit our weaknesses. Some of us feel inadequate at our work, many of us have feelings that we aren't masculine enough, and many of us feel tempted to return to old destructive behaviors.

In this program we have a renewal based on truth. We build upon solid reality rather than upon fiction. Denying the truth to ourselves always made us weaker and sicker than the facts themselves ever could. Viewing the facts from a new position of acceptance shows they aren't nearly as bad as we thought. Our sincerity with ourselves becomes a solid footing for growth.

My strength today is based upon a sincere relationship with myself.

Self-righteousness is a loud din raised to drown the voice of guilt within us.

—*Eric Hoffer*

A holier-than-thou attitude within us is often a sign of unconscious dishonesty. Who hasn't had the feeling of being superior to the angry outburst or the near-slip of another man—and then found himself in the very same spot the next day? What we least want to admit about ourselves is what we are most likely to feel self-righteous about.

Since our blind spots and self-deception leave us vulnerable to returning to old behaviors, we must attack them vigorously. The man we feel most self-righteous toward may be the man we could learn the most from. When we stop focusing on him, we may notice he touches our most sensitive area. We're all creatures of God and equals in God's sight. The ways we create inequality are the ways we fall short of God's wisdom.

I will use my self-righteous feelings to point me to my own blind spots.

Self-knowledge and self-improvement are very difficult for most people. It usually needs great courage and long struggle.
—Abraham Maslow

This is a simple program but it isn't easy. We cannot take the principles we learn and thereby possess them as if we were taking a class or reading a book. We need to live them. We can only get this program by participating with others who are also on the journey. Gradually we absorb it into every fiber of our being. This takes time and dedication.

The honesty required is sometimes frightening and painful. Any man who remains faithful to this program has great courage and deserves deep respect. But we do not have to wait long to begin receiving the rewards. New freedoms, good feelings, and friendships quickly develop, and we are promised in this program to continue growing and to receive more benefits throughout our lives. What rewards have come from our courage and struggle?

I will give much to my spiritual growth because it gives much to me.

Become nothing before God, learn to keep silent;
in this silence is the beginning, which is first to
seek God's kingdom.

—*Søren Kierkegaard*

So many devastating things can bring us to our knees. With experience we learn that pain and trouble are part of life. Most of us have fought against everyday realities as if they were our personal enemies. We accepted every challenge, thinking we had to be winners every time. Today we may feel broken by the loss of a love, by a disappointing job experience, or by our powerlessness over a loved one.

In our brokenness we find our true humanity. It is the beginning of our spiritual awakening. As men we thought surrender was a word for losers and weaklings. Living this program teaches us that accepting our brokenness opens us to a new kind of wholeness. After we acknowledge we are not in control of every event in our lives, and after admitting our addiction and codependency have controlled us, we come alive inside with the rich new experience of being a person.

God, help me today to learn the spiritual lesson contained in my frustrations and grief.

The wild geese do not intend to cast their reflection; the water has no mind to receive their image.

—*Zenrin poem*

There are moments which simply happen through no conscious intention or will on anyone's part. The image of an old woman with a peaceful face, the smell of smoke rising from a chimney on a chilly night, the knowing look of recognition from a friend as we make a comment, the special feeling of a touch. These are spiritual moments because they reach a deeper part of our being. They are like a sliver in time set aside which nourishes our souls and adds serenity to our lives.

We grow when we learn to notice these kinds of moments. In our willfulness, we have often missed them before because we simply were not open to anything we weren't already looking for. This world is so much larger than the human mind. In recovery, we can take time to admire the beauty reflected around us.

Today, I will let the rest of life intrude upon my mind. I will let myself be nourished by what comes along.

A man has made at least a start on discovering the meaning of human life when he plants shade trees under which he knows full well he will never sit.

—D. Elton Trueblood

Our lives are enriched by the contributions of those who lived before us. Many men and women gave more than they ever took from society, and now we enjoy the rewards. Some people were fired with a spirit to beautify the world and planted trees that will live for 200 years. Others wrote music that speaks to us from another generation, and others established a government that guides our principles of justice. They gave so much because they knew they were a part of their community and the world.

Most of us cannot make the great contributions that will make us famous, but we enrich our lives when we contribute freely to improving our community and the world. We do that when we simply say hello to our neighbor, when we serve on a volunteer cleanup committee for a local park, and when we do Twelfth Step work in the program. We too have beautified and contributed to the world, and that gives us a feeling of peace and self-respect.

Today, I will appreciate all that comes freely to me from others, and I will give what I can to make the world a better place.

I feel the more I know God, that He would sooner we did wrong in loving than never love for fear we should do wrong.
—Father Andrew

Love has often been called the first rule of a spiritual life. As we awaken to our new life in this program, we learn that all of God's creation is full of objects for us to love. A sunset repeats the creative energy at work in our world today. It appears briefly, invites our love, and slowly fades away, only to be repeated in a new form the next day. The color and markings on a little bug may inspire our love as may the smell of moist earth, the excitement of a Broadway musical, the craftsmanship of a well-made tool, or the look of warmth on a friend's face. These are all opportunities for us to let go and feel our love.

We men often feel awkward in expressing love. Perhaps we're so self-conscious and guarded that we brace ourselves against saying or doing anything that wouldn't look good. We're learning through our spiritual development to be more fervent lovers and less perfectionistic in love.

I will be renewed today each time I appreciate something near me.

Often our trust is not full. We are not certain that God hears us because we consider ourselves worthless and as nothing. This is ridiculous and the very cause of our weakness. I have felt this way myself.

—*Julian of Norwich*

Many men do not think they are worthy of recovery. Some of us even fight against our own progress. We can't seem to reconcile our low self-image with all the benefits recovery brings. This is not surprising when we see how many years we lived in self-abusive addictions. We had lifestyles in which we were treated badly by others, we abused ourselves, and we used and abused others. In our insanity, this sometimes felt masculine. Such a life does not prepare us to feel worthy of the good things in recovery. It is ridiculous to continue such pain simply because it's what we have known.

To turn this pattern around, we have to accept our Higher Power's view of us. Our Higher Power accepts us and sees us as deserving the benefits of recovery. We can get out of the way of our recovery by letting go of our unworthy feelings.

Today, I will be open to the benefits of recovery.

It is senseless to speak of optimism or pessimism.
The only important thing to remember is that if
one works well in a potato field, the potatoes will
grow. If one works well among men, they will
grow. That's reality. The rest is smoke.
— Danilo Dolci

We can get so mired in our pessimism and negativity! What is the point in it? We even get committed to our pessimism, and we challenge the world—or God—to give us reason for hope. In our pessimism, we don't notice we have chosen a negative place to stand. Recovery means loosening our grip on negativism. We are then free to do the work we need to do. We can slowly take the risk of believing that positive things will happen too.

Any man can see the results in his own life. When we work well at this program, when we are faithful to it, we do grow. We see this truth in one another's lives. The work is not always easy. We sometimes wish to avoid it or find a reason to not even try. But there is no doubt, when we look around us, that the effort is rewarded with fulfilling lives.

God, please remove pessimism from me so I may continue
my work.

That which is lacking in the present world is a profound knowledge of the nature of things.
—*Frithjof Schuon*

Most of us have very narrow, limited ways of understanding what happens to us. We are generally practical men, and if something goes wrong we immediately begin to think of how to fix it. We take a cause-and-effect approach to understand the events around us rather than a circular or symbolic approach. Perhaps we turn quickly to blaming instead of asking what is the meaning or the message in what is happening. We see our own experience as the center of events. We forget that our lives are only today's expression in a line of generations before us.

We become too self-satisfied with our ways of understanding the world. It may be comforting to think we understand what is going on. When we let go of that comfort and open ourselves to a more profound awareness, we enter the spiritual realm. Here we learn that facts are not enough to achieve truth. We begin to understand that love—in the form of connections with all of creation—is where we find the most profound meaning.

I am a part of the whole universe, and my relationship with my Higher Power will open me to profound knowledge.

Superficiality is the curse of our age. The doctrine of instant satisfaction is a primary spiritual problem.

—*Richard J. Foster*

As we have reached for instant cures, one-minute answers, and quick highs, we have developed lifestyles that foreclosed deeper possibilities. For instance, when we fail to stay and resolve conflicts in a relationship, we miss the joys of a renewed understanding. Our spiritual development comes in steps, small but meaningful increments that build over a period of time. Many of us have not been patient men and our newfound spiritual life is teaching us that the quickest, most efficient answer isn't always best.

Today, our greatest temptation may be to grab for the fast solutions rather than allowing time for small but important steps to occur. When we are frustrated, it will help to remember the difficulty may lie in our insistence on a quick answer. Sometimes simply being true to ourselves and standing as a witness while the answer develops are all that is asked of us.

I will have faith that time is on my side and it will teach me valuable things.

NOVEMBER

Music washes away from the soul the dust of everyday life.
— Berthold Auerbach

We may have spiritual experiences in our daily lives that we don't think of as spiritual. For many of us, music lifts us from the practical and mundane circumstances of our lives into communion with the universe. One man may like to listen to country music on the radio, another one might play the piano, and another may go to rock concerts. For each of us, music is a different world from the reasonable, hard data, task-oriented world we usually live in. Music touches our feelings and speaks to us in a special language. It brings us back to special times in the past, perhaps recalls a night of fun and excitement or a person we shared a song with. Music lifts our spirits and opens us to deeper feelings we weren't in touch with. Many of us meet our Higher Power through the music we love.

Today, I will make room for the restorative powers of music in my life.

Honesty is stronger medicine than sympathy, which may console but often conceals.
                                             —*Gretel Ehrlich*

We owe our brothers and sisters in this program our honest feedback. And we need the same honesty from them. There are times in meetings when it would be easiest to give someone sympathy and privately mutter to ourselves, "He isn't facing the bitter truth." That sympathy avoids a confrontation, but it doesn't give the healing medicine of honesty. In the same way, we may long, at times, for someone to give us warm strokes, and what they give instead is a bitter pill.

The most important thing we have to give one another is the truth of what we see and hear. We don't have to tell them what to do. We don't have to have all the right answers. But we do have the obligation to speak up about how things look to us. And we need to listen without defensiveness when others are honest with us.

Today, I will say what I see and hear. I will listen to other people's honesty with me.

*I, God, am your playmate! I will lead the child in
you in wonderful ways for I have chosen you.*
—*Mechtild of Magdeburg*

Our relationship with our Higher Power is not all
solemnness. Facing the pains and guilts and griefs of
our codependent relationships and our addictions
might lead us to think recovery is only serious business. Not so!

This program liberates us from the heaviness by facing it. We are not meant to stay stuck there. Recovery
teaches us to enjoy life. Our Creator has concocted a
world of many pleasures and delights to play in. As we
progress in our recovery we learn to let our hair down
and play. Some of us have become more able to enjoy
good-natured rough-housing with our children.
Maybe we have become more free to joke and banter
with friends. Our spiritual lives grow with good-
natured fun.

*I am grateful for the child who still lives in me. He keeps
alive my delight in the world.*

Much as I long to be out of here, I don't believe a single day has been wasted. What will come out of my time here it is too early to say. But something is bound to come out of it.
—*Dietrich Bonhoeffer*

These words, written by a man imprisoned for standing up against the Nazis, speak to us today about our own lives. We too long for release, and we cannot see where things will lead us. His spirituality is heroic; it inspires us. We do not know just where our lives will lead or what the outcome will be. But we can know our lives are taking us in the right direction. We make our choices today and stand up with all our energy for the honesty and dignity which this program provides.

We choose to trust life. In each tiny detail of this day we move forward, asserting our faith and seeking to know and do the will of a Power greater than ourselves.

I will open myself to the will of my Higher Power as I move forward on the path, living with my unrevealed future.

The struggle of the male to learn to listen to and respect his own intuitive, inner promptings is the greatest challenge of all. His ... conditioning has been so powerful that it has all but destroyed his ability to be self-aware.

—Herb Goldberg

Men strive to be successful with mechanical, physical, and powerful things. Some of us have succeeded in those supposedly "male" ways and others haven't. But whether we have or not, most of us have poured our energies into those directions and neglected the other way of being strong men. We may not have learned how to be gentle and helpful fathers, sensitive lovers, or men in tune with our own spirits and feelings. Many of us never learned to recognize what we feel.

Perhaps we were taught to stand up for ourselves. But have we learned to stand up for our right to have feelings? Do we stand up for our right to be learners and to make mistakes? Do we stand up for our right to be aware and to be the men we find ourselves to be, rather than what others tell us we should be?

I will become more aware of my inner self as a growing man on this uncharted journey.

The main thing in life is not to be afraid of being human.

—*Pablo Casals*

The "shoulds" of our lives can be found all around us. We should wear our seat belts. We should not cry. We should go to our meetings. These "shoulds" usually serve as good guides for us, but they can intrude upon us. If we give them power, they only condemn us and give no useful help. At times we jump toward the "should" because we don't have the courage to live with the insecurity of being human.

If someone at work gets an unfair shake, it takes courage to speak up and say what we think. We may have an impulse to reach out to a stranger, but it takes courage to do it. When an inner feeling emerges from our honesty, fear may prompt us to avoid it, and we need to call on our courage. That is how we fulfill the uniqueness of each of us.

I am alive as a man and a human being. I will not shy away from opportunities to express my humanity.

If the Great Spirit wanted men to stay in one place He would make the world stand still; but He made it to always change, so birds and animals can move and always have green grass and ripe berries, sunlight to work and play, and night to sleep.

—Flying Hawk

The American Indian's spiritual knowledge teaches that God has a rhythm and a benevolent purpose for the earth. How we relate to the changes which overtake us is central to our spiritual lives. With our overdeveloped will, we still fight change in many ways. We fight the aging of our bodies by an oversensitivity to our thinning hair and increasing grayness. We refuse to accept the end of summer by pouting and getting depressed about the cold. We try to hasten the time when our children are more independent and then hold them back when they get there. Peace comes with trusting the Great Spirit to bring changes in their natural progression. The extent of our willfulness affects our serenity—but not the progress of change.

God, help me accept the changes in my life.

Normally, we do not so much look at things as overlook them.

— *Alan Watts*

As we live our very busy lives we might say, "How full and rich my life is!" But are we stopping long enough to look, to take in experiences, digest them, and grow from them? Or is our attention always focused upon the next event? Are we running from one thing to another, never truly being present in the current moment?

For spiritual deepening, many of us men do not need to enrich the events in our lives as much as we need to simplify and quiet ourselves. We need to slow down and look at what is here. At a banquet, we might appreciate a few fine foods served in a tranquil atmosphere more fully than a lavish variety served in a frenzied atmosphere. For today, we are not able to stop the hectic pace of the world, but we can slow ourselves down and notice and reflect upon our experiences. Then they will have meaning and value for us.

Today, I will slow down. I will notice what my experiences are and give myself time to look.

Silence is the element in which great things fashion themselves together.
—Thomas Carlyle

Silence does not draw attention to itself. It is the ultimate in letting go and letting be. It is the opposite of the great dramatic event, so we easily forget silence is a basic means by which we grow. We live in a "can do" society that applauds a man of action who gets a job done. Perhaps we learned to think that being alone in silence is empty time with nothing happening.

In truth, some great things happen only by decisive action, but other great things happen only when we get ourselves out of the way and simply allow them to occur. It would be foolish to believe only in action and miss the benefits that come from quiet moments. When we withdraw from the hubbub of the world around us and quiet our minds, we are making room for great things to fashion themselves together.

Today, I will remember the importance of silence in my growth. I will set aside some of my busyness and be still.

Humility is just as much the opposite of self-abasement as it is of self-exaltation.
—Dag Hammarskjöld

In our struggles with self-hate and guilt, we may have thought we were humble—or perhaps even too humble. But self-abasement, which often alternates with feelings of superiority, is not the spiritual quality of humility that we strive for in our program.

With humility, we respect ourselves and our place in the universe. Humility is having ourselves in perspective, knowing we are connected to the whole world, accepting how small and powerless we are, and accepting the power and responsibility we have. With this spiritual feeling comes a sense of awe for the world we live in and a feeling of gratitude for the life we've been given.

The humility I feel today goes hand in hand with my self-respect and gratefulness for being part of life.

Nobody can give you freedom. Nobody can give you equality or justice or anything. If you're a man, you take it.

—Malcolm X

It does little good to complain about our wives or parents or lovers. We only accentuate our role as victims when we say, "I would be happier if she were different." "If he would just get off my back, I would act better." We each have a side which is loyal to the victim within. Some of us take comfort in acting helpless and being taken care of; some of us relish the power of being catered to; some of us wallow in self-pity. These patterns of thought retard our recovery and put a drag on our relationships. When we decide that we aren't willing to live this way any longer, we are ready to assert our independence.

Real emancipation can't come at someone else's initiative or as a gift. It can only begin from within, by saying, "I will take my independence." Then we begin to be responsible men because we own it on the inside.

Today, I will not wait for others to set me free. I will do what is within my own power to be a free man.

An ideal is a man's portrait of his better self.
—*Louis Binstock*

When in training for athletics, we use a daily routine to reach a peak condition. We stretch, lift weights, run, and do special conditioning to develop our bodies and skills for that big day of competition. It's hard work. Sometimes we hate it, but at other times we do it just because it feels so good. Then when the day of competition comes, we can depend on that practice. At a crucial moment there's not time to think about how we will respond. We just do it the way we learned and use our physical ability to carry us through.

In this program we go to our meetings, we work the Steps on a personal level, we develop a relationship with our Higher Power, and we keep in touch with our sponsor. Some days we may wonder if it's worthwhile, but most of the time the process is full and rewarding in itself. We make progress toward the ideal although we never achieve perfection. When the challenges or threats to our sobriety come, we have our conditioning within the program to carry us through.

In this day ahead I will remember that I am building myself to peak condition. I will be faithful to my "training program."

All men should strive to learn before they die
what they are running from, and to, and why.
—*James Thurber*

We are getting to know ourselves each day. We have learned some very important things about ourselves since the day we started our recovery. Most of us began learning by admitting our addiction or codependency. We saw how loyal we had become to a substance or a behavior. What seemed normal to us was actually distorted and unhealthy living. We didn't understand why we felt so confused and upset. Perhaps we didn't know what we were running to, or from.

Until we were faced with our powerlessness we couldn't know ourselves. We could not feel our void or pain until we had relinquished our old ways. We now can see our motives more clearly. When we have come face-to-face with ourselves, surrendered and stopped running, nothing else ever need be so frightening again.

I will let myself know where I am going today.

No one can get rid of the spirit of judgment by an effort of the will.

— Paul Tournier

In the past, we applied our wills and tried to bring about the changes we wanted. We may still unconsciously try to create self-improvement by an effort of will. But, as long as we do that, we continue the same circles of frustration and defeat we knew before recovery. The way to growth is in directions we cannot fully imagine for ourselves. We can become ready for change and then pray for help. The man who simply became ready to have God remove his judgmental attitudes was surprised to find God's answer was to make him more trusting of others and less judgmental of himself.

The wonders of recovery are miracles because we tried before and couldn't recover by ourselves. Miracles are surprises that come upon us because God's will for us is more creative and far-reaching in its renewal than anything we can think of.

Today, I pray that I may know the will of God and forgo my limited willfulness.

To wait for moments or places where no pain exists, no separation is felt and where all human restlessness has turned into inner peace is waiting for a dream-world.
—Henri J. M. Nouwen

Anytime we do a spot check on our anxiety or personal restlessness we will probably find some. As long as we are aware and alive we can expect to have some discomfort, some fear of loss, some doubt. Our program does not totally rid us of these pains. Perhaps our old ways sought absolute peace or escape through abuse of chemicals or food or gambling or sex, but the serenity we seek in our recovery comes through honesty with ourselves and acceptance of the incompleteness of our lives.

When we make room for the pain in our lives, we allow the river of our emotions to flow. It will carry us along to other feelings like happiness and peace. Conflicting feelings can exist side by side in our lives, and when we try to control true feelings of restlessness or pain, we dam the flow of emotions and block the pleasant ones as well as the difficult ones.

I am moving to a real world where I know and accept my feelings.

A wise man never loses anything if he have himself.

—Montaigne

As recovering men, perhaps we have learned more fully what it means to have ourselves because we know the extremes of losing ourselves. In the past we weren't honest with ourselves or others, we didn't have our self-respect, and our compulsive actions violated our values. In that condition, we were incapable of believing in ourselves or of standing up for ourselves. Some of us felt like phonies or nobodies.

In this program we pray for wisdom, and it comes to us as we take possession of ourselves. We develop a better match between our inner feelings and our outer actions. We become willing to make choices, and we are able to take a stand based on our personal feelings and hunches. The things we possess like our gadgets, our cars, or our audio equipment are just temporary. Our integrity, our selves, can never be taken from us.

Today, I am grateful for the growing feeling within that who I am and what I believe is acceptable to me.

You cannot devalue the body and value the soul—or value anything else. The isolation of the body sets it into direct conflict with everything else in creation.

—Wendell Berry

Our bodies are part of creation as much as trees, lakes, mountains, flowers, and animals. Part of our growth into full manhood is treating ourselves respectfully. It is a spiritual practice to be fully accepting, active, and alive physically.

We can no longer be content to be only spectator sportsmen in front of the television set. We need to get our own muscles moving. What we take in as food expresses the level of respect we feel for ourselves. Our sexual expressions reflect the value we feel for our own bodies and our partners'. Our spiritual feelings become part of all the basic details of our lives.

Today, I stand in God's creation as a physical body. My spiritual experience includes all the ways I care for and accept my body.

I always entertain great hopes.

—Robert Frost

In our honest journey, we must admit life is often difficult and painful. But these facts do not describe all of life, and they do not determine how we respond. The sun rises warm and bright after a cold and dark night. The open, generous smile of a small child reaches into the soft part of us all. To be strong and hardy men on this spiritual path, we must be truthful about the pain and unfairness in life while holding firmly to a belief in all the generous possibilities.

Surrendering to despair, we trade the uncertainty of options for the certainty of gloom. Then we might say, "At least I'm never disappointed this way." Life isn't filled only with difficulty and pain. It is also filled with people whose dignity and spirit rise above their circumstances. There are situations when great sacrifice or love and wisdom turn a problem into an opportunity and a strength. If we look at what has happened in our own lives and in those of others, we have ample reason to hope.

My own experience in recovery gives me great hope in what can be.

Archie Bunker: What's wrong with revenge?
That's a perfect way to get even.
— Norman Lear

When we are locked within negative, hostile thinking patterns, we go around in mental circles. What
seems perfectly rational to us at the time looks misguided and blind when we look back. Carrying a
grudge or a desire to get even with someone is a can-
cer inside us. It belittles us and holds back our spirit.

We break through our mental circles by revealing
our anger to others. We talk with other recovering
men and let them know the details of our resentments. We listen to their experiences and apply them
in our program. As long as we keep our thoughts and
feelings to ourselves, we only recycle the same thinking system. When we take the risk and talk to friends,
we build bridges that bring in new ideas.

I will not harbor my resentments within myself. I will talk
with a trusted friend so I can learn to let them go.

The most important function of art and science is to awaken the cosmic religious feeling and keep it alive.

—Albert Einstein

There is no need to be concerned about a conflict between science and the spiritual life. People have turned to the spiritual in many ways since the beginning of humanity. Some are tribal and primitive, some very emotional, some focused on ideas and philosophy, some centered on tradition. Perhaps in the very center of our humanness is a spiritual compass. When we disown that orientation, do we lose some of our humanness? This program did not invent the spiritual outlook. It only tells us recovery will come through awakening of the spiritual within us.

We are on an exploration. We give ourselves over to it and only discover where our awakening will lead as it unfolds. The Steps tell us to engage with the God of our understanding, to develop a relationship of trust, total openness and humility, and to improve the contact. As the center of our humanness is restored, we come alive and our daily tasks take on new meaning.

May I be awakened again to that cosmic feeling we all inherit.

*For the trouble is that we are self-centered, and
no effort of the self can remove the self from the
centre of its own endeavor.*

—William Temple

This quagmire of troubles we men were caught in
came, in part, from our best efforts to be self-
sufficient. The harder we worked to provide our own
cures, to control others in our lives, or to control ourselves, the more we fixed our attention upon ourselves. We could not see that the answers we were
using were actually part of the problem, not the solution.

Even today we may be partially caught in the folly
of this thinking. Whenever we think we see our problems and the answers clearly but don't open our incomplete selves to the wisdom of others, we are in
danger of intensifying our self-focus. When we have a
pattern of telling our fellow members the completed
stories of our pain only when our pain has passed, we
are maintaining our self-centered system. We can't lift
ourselves out of our self-centeredness. We can only
turn it over to our Higher Power and allow ourselves
to be released.

---

*I am grateful for the healing which comes when I stop
being so self-centered in my efforts.*

Without heroes, we are all plain people and don't know how far we can go.
—Bernard Malamud

It is useful for us to reflect on our heroes for a time. Who do we greatly admire? Are they men or women? Are they closely involved in our lives, or are they distant and beyond our ability to reach on a personal level? Can we feel hopeful and open enough about life to have heroes?

Our heroes inspire us to find the new edges of our growth. We see in another man or woman the qualities and values we admire. We find our own best parts, perhaps partly hidden or undeveloped, in the people we hold as heroes. For example, if we admire a television personality, we can learn about our own values by asking what we admire in him or her. If we admire a friend, we may see a trait we hold dear in ourselves. As we grow and change, our heroes are replaced by others who fit our maturing values.

As I think about people I admire, I learn about myself from them.

We shall not cease from exploration.
And at the end of all our exploring
Will be to arrive where we started
And know the place for the first time
—*T. S. Eliot*

Our spiritual path is like a search leading home. We carry within us a yearning for the ideal, the perfect acceptance and love from our fathers and mothers. We long for fulfillment of our dreams, we long to feel strong and capable, and we want to understand, to truly come into our own.

As we peel back the layers of our defenses, we find what we knew all along. On a deep level, we knew no man could be totally self-sufficient. Now we are coming back to it as if it's brand-new. The best images of our parents' love and acceptance of us are what we return to as models for how we can be. It is true we can never go home again. Yet our spiritual journey mysteriously leads us back to explore what we knew deeply all along.

I will make peace with my past and explore the deeper knowledge I've always held within me.

Self-respect is the fruit of discipline; the sense of dignity grows with the ability to say no to oneself.

— *Abraham Heschel*

Most of us have struggled with our self-esteem. We believed if we felt better about ourselves we could change some of our behavior. In recovery we found the reverse to be true. First our behavior changed, then our self-esteem improved.

Only after we stop doing things we don't respect can we hear and accept the goodwill of others around us. Then we see our value as men because we are upholding strong self-images by our actions. This is not easy to do. As we learn, we continue to say no to weak behaviors, and we are released to feel greater dignity.

Saying no to my negative behavior today will improve my self-respect.

It's the awareness, the full experience . . . of how you are stuck, that makes you recover.
—Frederick S. Perls

When we become aware of how far off our path we have strayed, when we see how cold and hard we were to someone we love, when we are no longer blind to our blindness—then we are touched by painful feelings. We feel guilty about the harm we caused. We grieve the lost moments and lost opportunities. We may feel angry with ourselves for our stubbornness. But even with our pain, we are worlds away from that blindness.

This new awareness is a spiritual place. It brings us back into contact with our Higher Power and makes us available to the words of wisdom and concern of others. It reminds us that no man can walk this path on his own power. We all must remain open and in contact with the healing relationships around us.

I pray for awareness today as my doorway to spiritual healing.

If the only prayer you say in your whole life is "thank you," that would suffice.
　　　　　　　　　　　　　—Meister Eckhart

"An attitude of gratitude," we sometimes hear, will help us on our path. There certainly are enough things for us to worry about, grieve over, and complain about. They have their place. But as we mature and no longer use addictive escapes, we learn that joy can exist side by side with grief. Gratitude is a tonic for our self-pity. Saying "thank you" actually opens us to receive more of life's blessings which sit there waiting for us to notice.

In a pleasant moment we can look around and say, "Aren't we lucky!" That's a kind of prayer, and it connects us with our Higher Power. No matter how painful or worrisome a day may be, we can be thankful for our growth. Gratitude is so simple we sometimes dismiss it while looking for a more complicated answer in our lives. We can say "thank you" for all the simple things like trees, cool air, food to eat, and love between people. It is a risk to be so grateful. Who will be in control? Perhaps God.

God, thank you for all that comes to me without my efforts.

The simplest questions are the most profound.
Where were you born? Where is your home?
Where are you going? What are you doing?
—Richard Bach

As we examine our personal answers to these simple questions, we find profound truths about ourselves. We may have been born in more places than the place of our biological birth. Some of us might say, "I truly was born the day I first felt the nurturing love of another person in my life," or "My life began on the day I stood up to my father." Most of us began new lives when we walked into our first meeting to begin recovery.

If we think about where our home is or where we are going and what we are doing as spiritual questions, we may find some comforting answers. Perhaps the place where we find rest, peace, and comfort is our home. That may be in a moment of meditation rather than in a physical place. If we are headed toward a manhood of self-respect, the problems of today are only challenges along the way. As we simplify our lives and let the truth be on the surface, we find profound meaning.

Today, I will keep my attention on the basics in my life.

Our job gives most of us a clear role.... Although we may feel relatively lost at home, we know who we are and what to do at work.
—Pierre Mornell

Most men have become well adapted to the workaday world. Even if our jobs seem like drudgery, they provide us with a place and a routine which define us. Many of us have welcomed the end of a weekend or a vacation because we could go back to our jobs and definite roles. This situation has many drawbacks. For one thing, if we are out of work, we may feel adrift. Furthermore, if we have defined ourselves only as breadwinners, we have probably missed the benefits of closeness in our families. Some of us have even said, "I feel like I'm nothing but a meal ticket."

A good job does have value, but we can also grow by giving more of ourselves in our less clear roles at home. It is healing to just "hang around" with our families and friends and to simply let relationships develop. The personal, familiar relationships that don't depend on jobs and roles let us be comfortably human.

I am thankful for the humanizing effect of my relationships at home.

*As with expeditions into the wilds when we have
endured storms and rapids, cold and sleet, and
sometimes lack of food, it is ultimately the good
things we remember, not the bad.*
—Sigurd F. Olson

In our daily lives we often take a very short perspective. We see what is worrisome today, what is
pressing hardest, or what is most frightening or confusing. Eventually, we may look back and have a totally different idea about what was truly important on
this day.

Let us take a moment now to remember what does
endure, what we value most, what counts in the long
run. For a brief quiet time we can let go of all the anxieties of this moment. During these few quiet moments, we will identify our tensions and then place
them totally into the hands of our Higher Power. This
is our time to let go of our worries and be refreshed. It
will provide a background of serenity for our day.

*Today, help me remember this corner of serenity as I meet
the tasks and activities on my path.*

A man cannot be comfortable without his own approval.

—Mark Twain

It is hard for many of us to learn to admit the wrongs we do. We have followed lifestyles that led us away from recognizing our true feelings. Remnants of this blindness continue into our recovery. In this quiet time we can deepen and nourish a relationship with ourselves. Facing our disapproval and admitting it lead us to comfort and self-respect. Right now we can ask ourselves, "What messages do I receive from myself? What is my Higher Power telling me? Do I sense some gut feeling? Am I true to my relationships with loved ones? Have I been open to the feelings of my spouse. Of my friends? Of my boss? Do I owe anyone an apology which I can promptly make?"

Some of us indulge in worry, fear, and anger beyond a useful or meaningful point. What can we do about these excesses of feeling? First, we admit them to ourselves and to others. Then, we trust our Higher Power for the outcome, and they will fall away.

Today, I will nourish a relationship with myself by facing my own disapproval and growing toward greater comfort.

DECEMBER

In the depths of winter, I finally learned that within me there lay an invincible summer.
—*Albert Camus*

Sometimes we suddenly see or sense opposite emotions within ourselves. The cold of winter presses in on us, and we may feel tested by its bite. Yet, when we think we cannot bear it a moment longer, we find a counterforce within, an inner reassurance that comes like a summer breeze and says we can do what we must. Perhaps it comes in a time of dark despair, and we realize that at least we've made it this far. We *are* pretty tough. In our deepest sadness about the loss of a love, we may find a more meaningful contact with our Higher Power.

The opposites in our lives may tempt us to fight them. One side may be very clear and obvious while the other side is hidden. When we are open, these extremes are spiritual teachers for us. As we think about life and our feelings today, what opposites do we find?

Today, I will remember that I have an invincible summer at the deepest part of winter in my life.

The management assumes no responsibility for what is found.

—Abraham Maslow

There are so many occasions when we would like to blame somebody—wife, child, parent, or "the management," for our feelings. When we get frustrated, overworked, or angry, we want somebody else to take responsibility. In truth, each of us has his own path and is responsible for his feelings. One man said that living alone made it clear to him that his wife wasn't creating his feelings. Until then he thought she was responsible.

This blaming and not taking responsibility keep a man in the role of victim. When we accept the difficult message that our feelings are ours to deal with and no one else's, self-improvement begins. We begin to walk the difficult but self-respecting path of spiritual awakening. We can do something about whatever hurts. Even in that awakening there are no guarantees that who we are will be totally what we want to find. Our only guarantee is that our Higher Power is with us to deal with the realities of our lives.

Today, help me be responsible for what I feel and do.

Sometimes I go about pitying myself, and all the time I am being carried on great winds across the sky.

—Ojibway

"Ah, poor me," we sometimes say, "I have to work so hard!" "I have so much stress!" "If only my problem with money would get better, then I could be content!" "I just don't understand women!" "Why can't my family have fewer troubles?" This attitude of self-pity is as ancient as humanity. The Ojibway recognized blindness to the spiritual path. Every man has problems and challenges, and life often is not fair. Self-pity becomes a stumbling block when we get so narrowly focused upon our problems. We forget we are a part of a whole throng of fellow pilgrims on this path. It helps to notice others beside ourselves who are seeking courage to live their lives.

Sometimes we reawaken our awareness of our Higher Power by seeing that we are "carried on great winds across the sky." We have many blessings; we are not alone. Often within problems we discover our greatest blessings.

God, help me find the spiritual path in the choices I make today. Help me turn away from self-pity.

"He doesn't talk to me," says a woman. "I don't know what she wants me to talk about," says a man.

—*Lillian B. Rubin*

We have often heard that it's better to be men of deeds, not words. In our relationships with other males, we have learned to do things together, work together, or play a sport together. But in our relationships with women, we often see the other side of this coin. If we haven't learned to express our thoughts and feelings, the women in our lives may request or demand that we learn now. There is nothing wrong with our not yet having this skill, and there is nothing wrong with women longing to talk with us.

A close relationship promotes talking, and revealing thoughts and feelings. Words, when we are honest, are ways of becoming clearer and being more personal. We have the right to stumble around with our words. We also have the right to feel unsure of ourselves or frightened of saying what we feel. That kind of fear is the excitement of being close to someone we love.

Today, I will express my feelings and ideas so others can know me better.

[A relationship] takes time and deeds, and this involves trust, it involves making ourselves naked, to become sitting ducks for each other.
—Eldridge Cleaver

When we were lost in our excesses, we were limited in our relationships. The history of our friendships and loves may be evidence of that. Many of us had a primary relationship with a substance or an addictive behavior, and people had only second place. Many of us were so lost in our codependency that our relationships were two-dimensional. We didn't know how to be there with our whole selves. In recovery our ability to relate to others changes slowly. We learn how to love like everyone else learned—only we are learning a little later.

We have to be willing to be vulnerable. We also must be willing to be accountable—willing to say to our loved ones, "You can count on me to never leave without saying good-bye." "You can count on me to be respectful of you." "You can count on me to tell you how I feel, even when it hurts." As we mature, with the help of the Steps, we also grow in our relationships with others.

Today, I will be true to my relationships.

All real living is meeting.

—Martin Buber

Sharing coffee with a friend or playing a game of golf with him provides a little relaxation, a little fun, and a chance to catch up on each other's lives. Such things are the meetings of life. Holding a small child on one's lap, even walking the dog are meetings too. They are relationships with other lives based on sharing time with one another.

Meetings—this sharing of time—can be with the full range of our existence. A tree, a lake, a mountain, the stars meet with us in solitude and enlarge our lives. Meeting is more than driving by. We meet a neighbor, a woman walking down the sidewalk, a driver in the next car. Each meeting inspires different responses in us. With some, we may be open and receiving; with others, fearful; and yet with others, we want to exploit and use. If all life is meeting, perhaps I do not wish to meet in the way I have been. The way I meet others changes me. Maybe I am missing something. I can have more life by making more contact.

God, please guide my awareness in this day to each meeting as it occurs so that I can make contact more fully.

Seldom, or perhaps never, does a marriage develop into an individual relationship smoothly and without crises; there is no coming to consciousness without pain.

—Carl Jung

We don't seek perfect relationships in marriage or in other places in our lives. What we seek instead are real and honest connections. Perfection has a picture-book form, but it has no depth and no personality. This means that sometimes we will get upset with others, or they will get upset with us. We need a basic commitment to stay in the relationship dialogue, to continue returning to it as long as both people are willing to work on it. Working through crises is how a relationship grows from simply being an idea to having its unique reality.

We will be frightened by the rough spots. We will wonder if there is something wrong with us or with the other person, or the relationship. We cannot escape such questions. To run from the difficulties cuts off the possibilities for growth. It is a frightening thing to become real, to come into consciousness.

Today, I pray for courage to remain honest and faithful to real relationships through the crises.

There are two equally dangerous extremes—to shut reason out, and to let nothing else in.
—Pascal

Some of the greatest scientific thinkers deeply respect the nonrational, and they aren't afraid to say so. Perhaps it is part of their genius. The nonrational inspires fun, creativity, a connection with others, and a feeling of reverence. Trying to contain our thoughts within reasonableness squeezes the life out of them. The simple beauty of color and form in a stone; the graceful, synchronized movement of a flock of birds; the miracle of understanding and loyalty in a friendship—these are truths beyond our ownership. We can feel these truths. We can be moved and inspired by them. We can never fully know their mysteries.

Our addictive natures have led us men to overemphasize reason and the control it promises. We've become reasonable while discarding the less controlled, creative, humorous, mysterious, and personal aspects of our lives. At this very moment we may be so focused on figuring out the reasonable answer to a problem that we are blocking the gut message which is also here for us.

I can appreciate rather than understand the mystery of life.

That it will never come again is what makes life so sweet.

—Emily Dickinson

Life seems to be a continuous pattern of getting committed to things and having to let go—falling in love and losing the one we love, developing a job skill and having to change careers, caring for our children and letting them go off into the world. This is the rhythm of life, and our spiritual growth teaches us to make peace with it. Participating fully in the rhythm is how we become whole men. As addicts and codependents, we used our gambling, overspending, drugs, sex, work, or caretaking of others to avoid the pain of making deeper relationships and to avoid the grief over losing them.

Avoiding commitments and staying uninvolved may keep us safe from risks. They also keep us near our dangerous old patterns. Our program works when we can freely let ourselves go. First, we commit to our recovery program with no reservations. Then, in our increasing sanity we gradually let ourselves go in other attachments. We know we face losses as part of life. We will have the strength to grieve them and move on.

God, give me the inner liberty today to let go of myself and care.

If you can just observe what you are and move with it, then you will find that it is possible to go infinitely far.

—*J. Krishnamurti*

"Boys don't cry" is bad training for males. Worse than that were ideas like, "Don't pass up a dare," "Nice guys finish last," "Be a good provider," "Be aggressive." Some of these ideas have some value, but problems came from adopting them as the only way to be. We thought we had to work at being the strongest, the best, the least vulnerable. Now we are learning how weak and fragile such thinking actually makes men. It sets us up to go to the extremes we found in our addictions and codependency.

Weakness isn't the alternative to this thinking. Developing our spiritual side, we see that we don't have to work at being what we already are. A man can be strong enough to show his vulnerability. He can choose the opportunity to advance a relationship with his child over the opportunity to advance his career. He can choose to pass by a challenge without shame because he doesn't wish to spend his energy there.

I will be stronger today by simply allowing myself to be true to my feelings.

The art of living lies not in eliminating but in growing with troubles.

—*Bernard M. Baruch*

Naturally, we wish to avoid pain and difficulty, but life experience and a measure of reflection show us that most of what comes our way is beyond our control. We'll never outwit all the possibilities for trouble, even if we live to be 100 years old. We have often failed to learn from trouble because we cast ourselves in the roles of passive men and victims. We pointed outside ourselves and said, "Look at what is happening to poor me!"

When we use trouble as our teacher, we develop the art of living. We are taking a spiritual approach, using our Higher Power as our guide. We can choose today to use our difficulties for our learning and growth. We might ask, "What can I learn from this experience about myself as a man? How can I use this to strengthen myself for the future?" Serenity develops, not by eliminating life's difficulties, but by having a reliable relationship with our Higher Power in the midst of it all.

With God as my guide, I will use whatever comes my way as an opportunity for growth.

I like a man with faults, especially when he knows it. To err is human—I'm uncomfortable around gods.

—Hugh Prather

We are more comfortable around a man who has faults and knows it. We respect such a man. So why do we have such a hard time admitting our own faults? This matter of honesty comes very gradually and only with hard work. We may have to force ourselves to admit a fault because we expect to feel unworthy. In fact, what we do feel after admitting a fault is peacefulness and self-respect. We may expect to be rejected and judged by friends, but usually friendships grow more solid when we admit our faults. A true friend does not need to trust that we will always be right, only that we will be honest.

At this moment are we being nagged by some fault? Is there something about the way we have talked to someone that doesn't seem right? Have we been unfair or dishonest? This is a program of progress, not perfection. So, to make progress we admit our imperfections, and as we do, we become more fully human.

God, in this moment when I feel my human mistakes, help me to be open to your love.

Let nothing disturb you. Let nothing frighten you. Everything passes away except God.
—*Saint Theresa*

Learning to detach may be the most demanding and difficult part of this program. Detachment means being filled with closeness and love toward someone, yet knowing we cannot fix or protect that person. It means we can be in emotional contact but don't have to react to someone else's issues. We respond from our own center with what is fitting for us. Being detached means we allow others to be in the hands of God because we cannot live their lives for them. Detachment gives us an inner calm, an acceptance of our limits, and the freedom to live our own lives with integrity.

Detachment is a skill in living, and like other skills, we can practice it. Gradually, it becomes a natural response. True detachment takes root and grows within us over a period of time as we deepen our relationship with the Steps and with our Higher Power.

Today, I turn to God as my eternal rock for strength in learning to become detached.

No matter how old you get, if you can keep the desire to be creative, you're keeping the man-child alive.

—*John Cassavetes*

Creation is the work of God. It is not given to most of us to be famous artists. But the spiritual experience of being creative is open to us when we take on a creative attitude toward what we are doing. We might do this on the job when we determine to do more than just get the job done. We may decide to have fun while we do what needs to be done, or we may decide to put our best spirit into the work before us. Some men find creativity in working with wood, others in coaching sports with children, someone else in cooking, and another in community service.

Being creative moves us toward wholeness as people. As we create on the outside, we are being created on the inside. The way in which we live every aspect of our lives is a creative, growing process and a partnership with God.

As I approach this day, I will have an attitude of creativity that will nurture the wondering child within me.

*My mother was dead for five years before I knew
that I loved her very much.*
                                        —*Lillian Hellman*

Each day it helps us to remember that we are always
changing. Whatever is most clear to us today or is
most prominent in our feelings—the difficulties we
may be having with parents, wives or lovers, the worries we have about our children—is a part of an unfolding of events we cannot foresee. Just when we
think we know exactly the direction things are going,
they surprise us with change. Relationships continue
to evolve and mature as we do. Even when separated
from loved ones, our relationships may improve because we continue to grow.

Our task for this day is to be honest with ourselves,
to be respectful to others, and to stay open to our
Higher Power. Continuing to go forward, we put one
foot in front of the other. We are changing internally,
and circumstances around us are changing too. We remain hopeful for the future because outcomes are in
the hands of God.

*I cannot predict the direction of my growth. I will simply
remain true to myself today and stay open for surprises.*

Be patient toward all that is unsolved in your heart/ And try to love the questions themselves.
—*Rainer Maria Rilke*

Patience with ourselves may be the first step toward patience with others. In getting to know ourselves, we don't find what we have expected. If we did, we would only be proving what we already knew. Sometimes growth comes in surprising ways. It may be in acceptance and learning to love what is unsettled or unclear within. Some of us men want to rush through our learning and push our growth too fast. Others of us want to have a strong sense of confidence in our relationships with others but always feel vulnerable. Some wonder why their fears suddenly rise without warning. Another longs to know why certain things happened to him in his youth. Our growth is not our invention. When answers come, they are gifts, and we do not control them.

In part, self-acceptance is to say, "Yes, I am a person with this question, this unsettled feeling. Being alive is to be actively engaged in knowing and loving my questions even when I find no answer."

God, grant me the peace that comes with loving the unfinished part of me.

The purpose of man's life is not happiness but worthiness.

—*Felix Adler*

When we pursue happiness as a goal for its own sake, we usually reach the opposite point of emptiness. Feeling happy is a by-product of other life experiences. Happiness comes and goes. We welcome it but cannot capture and hold it, nor can we create a recipe for achieving happiness.

We will lead far more successful lives pursuing other values which we do have control over, such as honesty, respect for others and ourselves, seeking loving relationships, and making a contribution to the well-being of others. We can accept unhappiness and difficulties without struggle when we know we are doing something that has greater meaning. Our Eleventh Step tells us we pray only for knowledge of God's will for us and the power to carry that out. This helps us focus on God's purpose for us. We can have an inner sense of joy knowing we are leading meaningful lives, even when we aren't having a particularly happy day.

I will seek the goals that make my life worthwhile and welcome happiness when it comes.

Ultimately, both parents and children are seen as individuals. For all their claims on one another, each is entitled to a life separate and distinct from the other.

—Francine Klagsbrun

The process of untangling the relationships between ourselves and our parents—as well as with our children—is a long-term process. Each of us came into the world helpless. As sons, we had no choice about relying on our parents. We reached manhood with a mixture of gratitude, guilt, and resentment. The same is true of our children. Those of us who are fathers began with an obligation to our children. We may now feel a mixture of commitment, fulfillment, and guilt.

No parent can teach a child everything he or she will need. We all do what we can to continue to learn and grow. We have lifelong commitments to each other—within reason. We are all trying to make our way as best we can. We each need to advance our own well-being and not destroy our lives for the sake of a parent or a child.

Today, I will be responsible for myself. Then I can be more responsible to others.

If I were given a change of life, I'd like to see how it would be to live as a mere six-footer.
—Wilt Chamberlain

It's human nature for us to wonder what life would be like in another man's shoes. No matter how good or bad we've had it, we like to consider those possibilities sometimes. While we were still in the trap of living with an addict or being one, some of us used a fantasy world as an escape from our circumstances. Perhaps it was the only option we knew.

Now we are in a program which liberates us and gives us hope. It's not an easy program, but it is simple. We're learning that when we have a relationship with our Higher Power and become accountable, we gain more options and can have hope. We can do interesting and rewarding things in our lives now that were closed to us before. Sobriety makes it possible for us to go forward into reality and leave fantasy for play.

Today, I am grateful for life in the real world that recovery has given me.

Faith is the bird that sings when the dawn is still dark.
                                    —*Rabindranath Tagore*

There may be many things in our lives that seem unsure or doubtful. Whatever our hope or personal need today, we are not given the knowledge that tells us how things will turn out. In the predawn darkness we don't know how the day will unfold. Sometimes faith is simply a matter of continuing with our program in the midst of our doubt. Then we can be certain that whatever direction events take, whatever pain or trial we must deal with, we will still have ourselves because we have been faithful today.

Ultimately, it is when we have ourselves and our integrity that we are on the recovery path. It is our faith that keeps us there regardless of the setbacks and personal moments of darkness we each must meet.

I will be faithful to my program, even in the darkest moment of doubt or fear, and it will carry me through.

He not busy being born is busy dying.
                                    —*Bob Dylan*

An old story has been told of men in the program asking an alcoholic who had a slip, "What Step were you working on at the time?" The man who slipped was not working on any Step, and that is part of how he lost his sobriety. The message of the story is that when we are not busy being born spiritually, we are losing ground. It is essential to always be focusing our attention on one of the Steps. Each time we work a Step again, we are at a new place in life, and the Step will inspire something new in us just as it did the first time.

Although we may know the program well, keeping it as our center protects us from being reactive to the events and pressures in our lives. We are less likely to feel overwhelmed by situations or react with shame or anger. As long as we live, we are in need of being renewed.

Today, I will choose one of the Steps and think about its meaning for me.

There isn't enough darkness in all the world to
snuff out the light of one little candle.
                                        —Anonymous

Our lives can be like a battle between darkness and light. The darkness might be in our moods when we wake in the morning with feelings of despair. Then we can turn to the light of a prayer for openness: "God help me feel your love and acceptance." The darkness is there when we are tempted to take advantage of a clerk who gives us too much change. Perhaps we tell ourselves, "Everyone does it, it won't matter if I do."

Then the light comes as we remember that this program demands rigorous honesty, and each choice for honesty promotes our growth. The darkness may be when someone we care about is hurt or in danger, and we think, "I have to step in to prevent bad things from happening." Then we turn to our Higher Power for strength to stay in the relationship, but not control it.

Today, I can take a leap of faith by choosing an action and accepting that one small choice for the light makes a difference—even in all the darkness.

*Loneliness is the way by which destiny en-
deavors to lead man to himself.*
—*Hermann Hesse*

We have an epidemic of loneliness among men in
our world. Everywhere, men are walking around as
though in plastic bubbles that prevent contact with
others. We are cut off from closeness with our brothers and sisters, our own children, our mates, co-
workers, and neighbors. We have learned to play the
role, be efficient, and look good. Do we dare let others
know how we feel? Will they look down on us? Will
they think we're strange?

All this has made us ripe for the diseases of addiction and codependency. Some of us have romanticized
the pain of loneliness and glorified it. We sought some
comfort for our pain, but we only perpetuated it.
Breaking through the barrier to let someone know us
can be incredibly difficult. Yet, just to say "I feel
lonely" to another person makes us slightly less alone.
Going to meetings and working this program provide
a way out. The greatest benefits of the program for
many of us have been recovery from loneliness and
the genuine relationships we have developed.

Today, I will reveal some of my feelings to another person.

*Celebration is a forgetting in order to remember.
A forgetting of ego, of problems, of difficulties. A
letting go.*

—Matthew Fox

A holiday presents us men with an opportunity to practice the letting go of this program. This is a special day to set aside our work and our routines, to put our problems and burdens on the shelf. Let us join with others who are also letting go on this day and celebrate. Maybe we can learn from them how they do it.

We may have been too compulsive on past holidays to celebrate. Or perhaps our holidays are clouded with painful memories. We might miss loved ones or we may recall disappointments or the chaos of earlier holidays. There is no need for perfection in our celebration. We can have some tension, or pain, and yet set it aside as we join with others for a special day.

Today, I will set my ego aside and let go of the usual things in my life in order to reach out to others and participate in celebration.

In the sphere of material things, giving means being rich. Not he who has much is rich, but he who gives much.

—*Erich Fromm*

Material possessions have great significance in our world. Not only do we strive to own a special car, electronic gear, and far more clothes than we need, but we also think in terms of possessing a girlfriend, or our health, or happiness, or things that cannot be owned. Some of us have become addicted to buying and owning things. This gimme-gimme mentality affects us all and, rather than enriching us, it impoverishes us. Tangible things enrich us only when we use them and share them to improve our lives and the lives of others. We don't need to be wealthy to share what we have with others. It is the sharing that nourishes us and builds bridges between us.

Wise people have known for thousands of years that a man's spirituality is deeply affected by his relationship to his possessions. When we respect what we own as a gift from God and share it with others, we grow richer spiritually.

I will hold my possessions loosely and with respect so they can be used well and shared.

He who knows how to be poor knows everything.
—*Jules Michelet*

Letting go is one of the simple yet profound spiritual tasks taught by many of the world's religions. Knowing how to be poor means knowing how to have a full and rich life without a dependent relationship with material wealth, food, chemicals, or sex. It means not relying on the props in life like expensive clothes, a prestigious job, or a sporty car, but relying only on the basics. Knowing how to be poor is knowing we are not in control and not wasting our serenity in trying. It means being completely honest in all things. It means knowing life is neither easy nor free of pain.

Learning how to be poor is learning how to let go of all the essentials and appreciating the simplicity that endures. We don't automatically know how to do that, but we can learn.

I don't expect to know everything, but my Higher Power can guide me and show me how to let go.

Try not to become a man of success.
Rather become a man of value.
                                        —*Albert Einstein*

The marketplace and fashion entice us in countless ways to indulge our individual pleasures. Some say that success will be with the man who follows those seductive beckonings. Even sacrificing long hours by working two jobs to become a financial success or to achieve high career goals can be self-centered activity. It may be time and energy spent seeking power and glory at the cost of time with our family and friends— time for enjoying each other and growing. Sadly, external success leads to superficial pleasure but never to peace within ourselves.

However, when we pursue the values of honesty, humility, and service, we will find enduring self-respect and close friendships. This path provides a genuine experience of life's greatest rewards rather than the glitter of passing excitement.

Today, I will strive toward the greater values rather than superficial successes.

He is a man whom it is impossible to please,
because he is never pleased with himself.
                                                              —*Goethe*

Many of us grew up trying to please our fathers and feeling we never got the approval we needed. Perhaps our fathers couldn't feel pleased with themselves. Now it is time to take stock of ourselves and ask whether we are perpetuating the pattern in our own lives. If we still feel unhappy with ourselves, we may never be satisfied with anyone else either. Spouses, children, bosses, even the parking lot attendant may receive the brunt of our self-disapproval. We don't totally change these patterns in an instant. We change them one day at a time.

Today, we have before us a small piece of the future. We can begin by treating ourselves decently. Maybe we can't feel a strong sense of personal approval yet, but we can give ourselves some basic respect. We can start by remembering we have the love of God. We can affirm at least one positive thing about ourselves. After some positive reflection, we will have more to give to others.

Today, I will give myself approval for at least one thing.

Our greatest glory consists not in never falling,
but in rising every time we fall.
—*Ralph Waldo Emerson*

After we get a new understanding about ourselves we think, "Now I will never have to make the same mistake again!" But our lessons are usually not that easily learned. We have to get them into our muscles and bones as well as our heads. Some of us have to learn how to be kind; others, how to be good listeners or how to stand up for ourselves in many different ways. Every new situation calls on a little different way of knowing, and perhaps we have to fall a few times in the learning.

The most important asset in our lives is the faith to get up again and continue. We must accept our imperfections. Each time we fall and with each mistake we make, we're vulnerable to doubting and losing faith. By rising again, we make progress in our learning and continue to become better men.

Today, I will have faith, even in the midst of my mistakes.

When we are reduced to our last extreme, there is no further evasion. The choice is a terrible one. It is made in the heart of darkness ... when we who have been destroyed and seem to be in hell miraculously choose God!
—*Thomas Merton*

There are many ways we benefit from a life crisis. Perhaps none of us could achieve true adult maturity—or a relationship with God—without having the foundations of our lives shaken. One of our pathways to crisis was the willful pursuit of control in our codependent and addictive lives. Our lifestyles were extreme, the consequences were extreme, and our surrender had to be absolute.

Most of us are surprised by how our weaknesses can turn to strengths. When our defiant wills led us to the utter bottom of our despair, we finally turned to a Power greater than ourselves and found a new way to live. This spiritual story is told in endless variations in our meetings, and it is renewed in small ways every day in each of our lives.

God, lift my defiant willfulness from me and renew my day.

Dawns another year,
Open it aright;
Thou shalt have no fear
In its fading light.

—*Joseph Krauskopf*

New Year's Eve is a good time to reflect upon the closing year and set our direction for the year ahead. This day reminds us that every day of the year is lived just one at a time. Looking back, we can see a year's change in ourselves. We see the progress we have made as men on our journey. Perhaps we see how much stronger we are emotionally. Maybe we see relationships that have developed because of our growing ability to love. Certainly all of us have some things we regret and some changes we mourn. They too have their place today.

As we begin the coming year, let us review our relationship with each of the Steps. We may perceive aspects of our program that call for more attention. One or two particular Steps may speak to our needs at this time or may have been overlooked in this past year. On this last day of the year, we can again turn our lives and will over to the care of a loving God.

I look to the new year with a renewed commitment to the Steps.

INDEX